HONESTY MORALITY & CONSCIENCE

JERRY WHITE

NAVPRESS

BRINGING TRUTH TO LIFE
NavPress Publishing Group
P.O. Box 35001, Colorado Springs, Colorado 80935

The Navigators is an international Christian organization. Our mission is to reach, disciple, and equip people to know Christ and to make Him known through successive generations. We envision multitudes of diverse people in the United States and every other nation who have a passionate love for Christ, live a lifestyle of sharing Christ's love, and multiply spiritual laborers among those without Christ.

NavPress is the publishing ministry of The Navigators. NavPress publications help believers learn biblical truth and apply what they learn to their lives and ministries. Our mission is to stimulate spiritual formation among our readers.

© 1979 The Navigators
Revised edition © 1996 by Jerry White

Library of Congress Catalog Card Number: 95-50990
ISBN 08910-99425

Some of the anecdotal illustrations in this book are true to life and are included with the permission of the persons involved. All other illustrations are composites of real situations, and any resemblance to people living or dead is coincidental.

Unless otherwise identified, all Scripture quotations in this publication are taken from the *New American Standard Bible* (NASB), © The Lockman Foundation 1960, 1962, 1963, 1968, 1971, 1972, 1973, 1975, 1977; the *HOLY BIBLE: NEW INTERNATIONAL VERSION*® (NIV®), copyright © 1973, 1978, 1984 by International Bible Society, used by permission of Zondervan Publishing House, all rights reserved; *The New Testament in Modern English* (PH), J. B. Phillips Translator, © J. B. Phillips 1958, 1960, 1972, used by permission of Macmillan Publishing Company; *The Living Bible* (TLB), © 1971, owned by assignment by the Illinois Regional Bank N.A. (as trustee), used by permission of Tyndale House Publishers, Inc., Wheaton, IL 60189; the *Amplified New Testament* (AMP), © The Lockman Foundation 1954, 1958; and the *King James Version* (KJV).

White, Jerry E., 1937-
    Honesty, morality, and conscience / Jerry White.
       p.   cm.
    Includes bibliographical references.
    ISBN 0-89109-942-5
    1. Christian ethics. 2. Honesty. I. Title.
BJ1251.W54 1996
241—dc20   95-50990
                                            CIP

Printed in the United States of America

2 3 4 5 6 7 8 9 10 11 12 13 14 15 / 00 99 98 97

FOR A FREE CATALOG OF
NAVPRESS BOOKS & BIBLE STUDIES,
CALL 1-800-366-7788 (USA)
or 1-416-499-4615 (CANADA)

CONTENTS

To Mary,
my wife, companion, and friend;
and Stephen, Katherine, Karen, and Kristin,
my children,
who have taught me truth of life and honesty

FOREWORD

As a professor of Christian ethics, I have through the years read many learned volumes dealing with the deep theological and philosophical issues of morality. But I cannot remember a more helpful, down-to-earth discussion of behavioral specifics than this one by Jerry White. Taking the Word of God as his norm, he applies its absolutes to everyday problems and does so with illustrations that make abstract principles both concrete and conscience-probing. He shows how biblical standards, admittedly inflexible and demanding, can be worked out in business, the home, education, and yes—in church!

In a day of ethical confusion, this book will, I trust, be used of God to remind Christians that their lifestyle ought to be qualitatively different from that of our relativistic society. Only by putting into practice the God-sanctioned directives which Jerry White explicates can we who are professed biblicists become salt and light amid twentieth-century decadence and darkness.

—Vernon C. Grounds
President, Denver Conservative Baptist
Theological Seminary

PREFACE

Our couples' Bible study was cruising along smoothly in Philippians 2: nice thoughts, generalized comments, spiritual conclusions, insightful analysis, intellectual questions — all so very acceptable.

Finally, John, a banker, could contain himself no longer. "I feel like a hypocrite!" he blurted out. "How does all this spiritual stuff work in real life? It's not working for me. I go to work and do great for ten minutes and then I act like everyone else. By Friday I'm just one of them. I want to help people, but my managers say my job is money first and people second. I don't even feel like a Christian. Something is wrong!"

Our group wasn't quite the same the rest of the evening. The real world had smashed our spiritual reverie. We all tried to figure it out with John. We discussed how to relate Scripture to life in the world, yet the Bible did not seem to spell out *specifically* how to live in the banking profession. And John was torn by the gap he saw between biblical principles and what he felt he had to do to survive in his job.

That is what this book is about—the scriptural principles of honesty, morality, and conscience applied to those areas of life where a specific rule book was never written. It is a guide to help you handle the "gray" issues that confront you daily by using the Bible and your conscience, and by depending upon the Holy Spirit.

I am convinced that God has given us everything we need to face the kinds of moral questions and issues treated in this book—understanding the conscience; overcoming peer pressure; dealing with questionable business ethics; the special challenges of maintaining honesty in the home, in church, and in school; being honest with ourselves; maintaining sexual morality; and developing personal convictions in all these areas. It is from this confidence in God's provision that this book was written.

These issues were stimulated significantly by responses to the book *On the Job* written by my wife, Mary, and me, and to public seminars I conducted on the Christian and work. Many of the problems people were facing were not matters of job satisfaction, but were of an ethical and moral nature. Then I realized that the basic principles of honesty and conscience apply to much broader issues than business and work. In fact, they penetrate every area of life.

Many have contributed to this study, but special thanks are due to my wife, who edited the entire manuscript, to my secretary, Karla Boaz, who laboriously typed each draft, and to Adam Holz who assisted in the revision.

Additionally, four couples were the source of special encouragement and stimulation during the year this book was written—Rick and Sharon, John and Paula, Steve and Beth, and John and Nancy.

Chapter One

THE DILEMMAS OF HONESTY OR THE PROBLEM DEFINED

---∾---

"Guilty!"

The word sent chills up his spine and made his hands tremble.

The judge continued, "Guilty on all counts—lying to your wife, cheating on your income tax return, and stealing from your employer."

He sprang to his feet and screamed, "That's not true! I can explain every. . . ."

"Silence!" the judge interrupted. "The verdict stands. You will be held for sentencing." He pounded his gavel sharply.

Bill bolted upright in bed. His hands were moist. His pillow was damp with sweat.

"Bill! What's wrong?" asked his startled wife.

"Nothing. Just a bad dream."

Even sleep would not allow Bill to escape the issue. For the fifth time the crazy dream had wakened him. Each time he carefully reasoned through each point. The IRS thing, for example—it was perfectly legal. He had checked it with a tax lawyer. Of course, the matter of the travel expense reports was still a question. But, what of it? That trip had been a tough one. He deserved something extra.

But as he lay awake, a sickening feeling began to fill his body. *I did lie and I did cheat,* he thought. *But what can I do? It's done and I can't change it.*

What should Bill do? Had he really lied and cheated, or was his conscience simply playing tricks on him? Even if he had cheated, wouldn't it be best to forget it and start over?

What about the rest of us? Various dilemmas of honesty, morality, and conscience confront us daily. We read the Bible and find no clear-cut, direct answers for many of the questions. We face situations that seem to have no pragmatic answer. Yet we know there *is* a right and wrong. Furthermore, we realize that even Christians make decisions in these areas based on the thinking and habit patterns of the nonChristian world.

Let's look at actual dilemmas that some have faced in this area. Consider how you would respond in each situation.

CASE STUDIES

Case No. 1. A politician in a Western city won his party's nomination in a primary election. Shortly afterward several people accused him of misrepresenting his educational background. He had said he had a doctorate, they alleged, when he had not completed his work for it. Later he confessed that he had allowed people to call him "Dr." although he did not have the degree. He also admitted he might have written at some time that he had a Ph.D. He subsequently was forced to withdraw from the race.

Was this really dishonesty by misrepresentation? Was the controversy really necessary, since the degree was unrelated to the office? Was it a serious enough offense that he should have withdrawn?

Case No. 2. A teacher in a small town received a salary

below industry standard. Because of this, he would stock up on cheaper goods in a nearby city when he had the opportunity. One of the townspeople reprimanded him, saying that since the town paid his salary it was only right that he give his business to the merchants there.

Did the teacher act unethically? Should he purchase goods in the town to foster better relationships and maintain a Christian testimony among the townspeople?

Case No. 3. A church board was meeting to discuss the sale of bonds for a new building. The bonds were financed through a reputable bonding company. The church could sell the bonds in any state in which the bonding company was registered. As the church board met, they discussed at length whether they should sell a bond to someone who resided in a state where the company was not registered. One possible solution, practiced by a number of investment companies, was to have the buyer drive across the state line to conduct the transaction. This would have met the requirements of the law.

But would this be right? Would it be stretching the law? Could a business do this, but not a church? A representative of the bonding company had described the plan as "the right way to do a wrong thing." Legally it would pass. But ethically it would not. Should the board reject the plan?

Case No. 4. A pastor of a Spanish-American church frequently had illegal aliens in his congregation. If he turned them in to the authorities, he would not be able to give them the spiritual help they needed. But if he did not, he would be violating federal law.

Should he tolerate the situation, justifying his silence by pastoral confidentiality? Should he try to persuade the aliens to turn themselves in? What would happen if he was caught harboring aliens?

Dilemmas of ethics and honesty without clear-cut answers are legion. But that is where we live—in a real world with real problems that do not fit a simple "do and don't" list. How can a person get direction for these areas?

DEFINITION OF TERMS

When a word is used, each of us immediately forms a mental picture of what that word means. But often we function on differing definitions without knowing it. Words such as *morality*, *values*, and *ethics* can mean different things to different people. Unless we clearly define what we mean by these words, the possibility of miscommunication exists.

Imagine an employment interview where the company representative says, "Our company operates with a high degree of morality and integrity. You need to be aware of that before you consider joining us." When he says "morality," is this company rep speaking of how each employee treats the company (for instance, personal use of company supplies is not allowed)? Or is he speaking of how the company treats outsiders (for example, customers are to be treated fairly)? Depending on a person's background and belief system, it could mean any of these.

Thus, we need to define terms. The basic definitions given here will be expanded later in the book.[1]

Ethics encompasses the broad science or teaching of how to live a good life in the context of one's society or culture. It incorporates the accepted standards of the community as well as the personal conduct of individuals in that community.

Morality emphasizes the attributes of those who live this good life. Their conduct and character are excellent — defined both by their community and their personal religious beliefs. The moral person displays:

■ *Integrity*, the state of wholeness, consistency, and sincerity, with no deception or pretense.

- *Honesty,* the absence of lies, crookedness, deceit or fraud. Honesty is truthfulness, sincerity, and frankness.
- *Conscience,* the inner compass that helps navigate the moral areas of life.

The definitions are influenced by the values that we put into them—from society, family, Scripture, and religious beliefs. With this in mind, let's expand the basic definitions by exploring the roots of these words.[2]

Ethics: Derived from the Greek word *ethos.* In the plural form it means manners. It refers to rules or principles of conduct; a code of morality, a system of conduct; the branch of philosophy dealing with values relating to human conduct, with respect to the rightness and wrongness and to good and bad motives and ends of such actions.

Honesty: From the Latin word *honestos.* Related to *honos,* which means honor; the state of being credible, virtuous, upright, sincere, truthful.

Morality: From the Latin root *mores,* meaning customs, manners, character. It is excellence in conduct, virtue, or character; a conformity to the rules of right or virtuous conduct; virtue in sexual matters, chastity.

Conscience: From the Latin word *conscientia.* Con- meaning "together with," and *scientia* meaning knowledge. It is an inner awareness of what is good or bad, internal recognition of the moral quality of one's motives or actions; the source of moral judgments; an inhibitor to actions that are perceived as wrong.

Integrity: From the Latin *integer*. It is a state of wholeness (as in the word integral from mathematics),
sound, complete, uncorrupted, innocent, and virtuous; usually applied to a person's actions and intent.

THE SPREAD OF DISHONESTY

It seems easy enough to say, "Of course everyone can be
honest—at least most of the time in the big things." But
why not all of the time, and in little things also?

Consistent honesty doesn't happen easily, even among
Christians. In business, in the home, and in the classroom,
honesty is not simple. We slip into "white" lies and half-
truths almost automatically.

Joan Beck of the *Chicago Tribune* writes, "Lying is commonplace in our society—sometimes for what may seem
the best of reasons, often for personal gain, almost routinely
for social or business convenience ('Tell him I'm in a meeting')."[3] We cannot assume that honesty is a way of life in
our country—or in our churches. The forces of society have
subtly squeezed us into new definitions of honesty, morality,
and ethics. Absolutes of right and wrong have largely dis-
appeared and have been replaced by a fuzzy, gray fog of
inconsistent moral choices.

Perhaps we can all see ourselves in Mark Twain's story:

When I was a boy, I was walking along a street and
happened to spy a cart full of watermelons. I was
fond of watermelon, so I sneaked quietly up to the
cart and snitched one. Then I ran into a nearby alley
and sank my teeth into the melon. No sooner had I
done so, however, than a strange feeling came over
me. Without a moment's hesitation, I made my
decision. I walked back to the cart, replaced the
melon—and took a ripe one.[4]

Or can we follow the example of the famous baseball player, Ted Williams?

> When Ted Williams was forty years old and closing out his career with the Boston Red Sox, he was suffering from a pinched nerve in his neck. "The thing was so bad," he later explained, "that I could hardly turn my head to look at the pitcher." . . . For the first time in his career he batted under .300, hitting just .254 with 10 home runs. He was the highest salaried player in sports that year, making $125,000. The next year the Red Sox sent him the same contract.
>
> "When I got it, I sent it back with a note. I told them I wouldn't sign it until they gave me the full pay cut allowed. I think it was 25 percent. My feeling was that I was always treated fairly by the Red Sox when it came to contracts.
>
> "I never had any problem with them about money. Now they were offering me a contract I didn't deserve. And I only wanted what I deserved."
>
> . . . Williams cut his own salary by $31,250![5]

Would you do that? Was it honesty or foolishness? In our society such honesty is rare. Yet it is basic to Christian living and crucial to the moral life of our country.

Clare Boothe Luce, former congresswoman and ambassador, has along with many others expressed great concern about the decline of moral standards:

> Under the impact of science, religion has lost its social authority. Under the impact of technology, family life has disintegrated. The automobile, the radio, TV, etc., have destroyed parental control over the young. The process, which has taken more than a century, would seem to be irreversible.

Our educational system has long since abandoned the teaching of morals, or what is now called in academe "value judgments."

Today, ever-growing numbers of individuals feel fewer and fewer inner restraints or inhibitions against disobeying any law or moral code that interferes with their private desires or impulses. As the social stigmas that were once attached to lawbreaking and deviation from the traditional morals grow weaker, the distinction between liberty and license becomes more and more blurred in the mind of the individual. Pleasure and profit become the only guides to personal conduct. "The law" is seen as an enemy to be destroyed or outwitted. In the end, the only "sin" is "getting caught."

. . . If our democratic form of government continues for another two decades to fail in the discharge of this responsibility [maintaining social stability], it is bound to collapse, and our people are bound to turn to some other form of government that offers the promise of restoring order.[6]

How can a Christian make moral and ethical decisions in areas where society has erased restraints? We can be confident that the Bible presents workable answers to our moral dilemmas, and guidelines for living honestly. And in God's Word we discover that complete honesty is His commandment for us: "Behold, Thou dost desire truth in the innermost being" (Psalm 51:6); "Therefore, laying aside falsehood, speak truth, each one of you, with his neighbor" (Ephesians 4:25).

The very discussion of honesty, morality, and conscience implies some set of absolutes or standards by which we judge our actions and thoughts. But we encounter a serious problem. *The world has changed.* Increasingly, there are no agreed upon absolutes. Our moral base is rapidly fading into history. We now live in world of relativism. We live in a society that has been overtaken by secularism. Its central tenet is not religious—or even moral. Some would say that we are living in a post-Christian or postmodern world. But what does that *mean*? Are serious issues at stake? A significant change in moral and ethical thinking over the last three decades is revealed by statistics of crimes of violence, sexual beliefs, standards of behavior in business, and the content of the visual media.

Secularism rejects any religious content in the mainstream of our society. Postmodernism rejects belief or faith in absolutes of any kind. This combination results in the belief that we are in a post-Christian age.

The most visible result of this breakdown in belief in absolutes is a deep and pervasive relativism—a belief that there are no standards that comprise a norm. At best, ethical standards are seen as useful in conducting business. Thus, a business person may act honestly not because he values honesty or truth, but because being honest is pragmatic and useful to achieve his ends. At worst, right and wrong are defined only in the eye of the beholder. This results in perverse logic, which reasons, "It might be wrong for you, but it's okay for me." Ethics or moral behavior are thus reduced to pure subjectivity, more often than not based upon how we *feel* about a given issue. Right and wrong, in any absolute sense, have been taken captive by feeling. Such logic cannot be critiqued by a standard of truth, because it does not recognize the authority of any truth outside itself.

It would be easy to presume that these changes have not permeated Christian churches or people. But they have. They are a part of the unseen force of culture that shapes the practical belief systems of young people. The unstated assumptions of secularism and relativism are an integral part of their thinking. Therefore, the discussions of this book are not easily pursued without both a recognition and a rebuilding of these inherited cultural values. To accept biblical statements on a subject requires an acceptance of the Bible as a reliable authority. This is difficult in a relativistic world. Thus discussion of these issues is pointedly counter-culture.

Notes

1. My thanks go to Donald McGilchrist for many of the ideas in this chapter, which were stimulated by interaction with him.
2. *Random House Unabridged Dictionary*, 2nd edition, newly revised and updated (New York: 1993).
3. Joan Beck, "Lying Wastes Energy, People's Trust," *Colorado Springs Gazette Telegraph*, 9 April 1978.
4. Mark Twain, as quoted in *Reader's Digest*, August 1977, p. 91.
5. *Bits and Pieces* (Fairfield, N.J.: The Economics Press), September 1977, pp. 12-13.
6. Clare Boothe Luce, "If Present Social Trends Continue, Democracy 'Is Bound to Collapse,'" *U.S. News and World Report*, 5 July 1976, pp. 65-66.

Chapter Two

YOUR CONSCIENCE— FRIEND OR FOE?

———————— ∾ ————————

Willie, in the comic strip *Moon Mullins*, is slumped in a chair in front of a TV set, coffee cup resting on his pot belly. As he flicks his cigar ashes in his coffee cup, he says, "You're awful quiet this morning, Mamie."

"I've decided to let your conscience be your guide on your day off, Willie," Mamie replies.

In the next picture Willie is outside surrounded by lawnmower, rake, and hoe, and is frantically washing the windows. "@!** Every time I listen to that darn thing," he mutters, "I end up ruinin' my relaxin'!"[1]

That is how many people view their consciences—as a fun-killer, an irritating voice warning them not to do something, an unexplainable feeling to be repressed, tricked, or ignored.

The conscience speaks at the most awkward times. It unsettles the best thought-out plans. It prevents restful sleep. Years after an act has been committed or a word spoken, the conscience persists in reviving the memory of that deed. A day rarely passes without the conscience attacking some issue of inner thought or outward action.

Most people would like relief from this persistent voice.

But for a Christian, the conscience can be the most valuable resource, next to the Bible, in determining God's direction in any situation.

On a beautiful Saturday morning one summer I was sitting in the back yard reading and studying a passage in my Bible. My wife, Mary, returned from a grocery shopping trip, so I ambled to the front to help her carry the bags into the house. On a previous trip we had bought a watermelon that was spoiled, so she was to have exchanged it for a fresh one. But she informed me that the produce manager had refused to allow her to return it.

I started grilling Mary as to why he wouldn't grant a refund or an exchange. Anger started welling up inside me. The more we talked the angrier I became. Finally I picked up the phone and called the store. As soon as the produce manager answered the phone I began firing questions at him. Soon I was giving him a generous "piece of my mind." After venting my anger I hung up the phone.

We finished unpacking the groceries and I headed to the back yard to resume my Bible study. I sat down and tried to read. But my mind was a blank and my stomach in knots.

I tried to ignore the feeling. I began to realize my reactions and my conversation with the manager were unchristian and dishonoring to the Lord. *But I was absolutely right*, I reasoned. *He should have exchanged it.*

I tried to concentrate, but began arguing again with myself—or whoever was my tormentor. I began to sweat, but not from the sun.

Finally I put down my books and stalked into the house. I knew my conscience would not let me rest until I called the produce manager and apologized. I dialed the number, thinking, *Maybe he won't be in.* But then I thought, *He has to be in or I'll have to spend a whole day in misery!*

"Hello, Mr. Clark. This is the man who called you a little while ago about the spoiled watermelon." *All this about one dumb watermelon and a few angry words. How ridiculous,* I thought.

"Mr. Clark, I am a Christian and it was entirely wrong for me to treat you the way I did. I want to apologize for what I said." Now I was really sweating and nervous. But I knew this was the right thing to do.

I expected a curt acknowledgment or rebuff. Instead he said, "I'm a Christian too. I take a lot of things from people so I just listen and do the best I can. Thanks for calling."

After a few minutes of talking, I hung up the phone. A load was lifted off my shoulders. Why?

Conscience. My conscience told me my attitude and speech were wrong, and persisted until I obeyed and corrected the situation.

But how did I know my conscience was right? What if it was overly sensitive and duped me into an action that was unnecessary or awkward and embarrassing? And what about other times when I did something wrong and my conscience said nothing?

We all experience the struggle of knowing when to follow our consciences. We may have questions like these:

- How can I be certain my conscience is speaking and that I am not simply experiencing a response conditioned by my family, my education, and my church background?
- Is the conscience biblical?
- Can Satan use it?
- Is the conscience of a Christian the same as that of a nonChristian?
- What if God's Word and my conscience are in conflict?
- Can I train my conscience to respond differently?
- If my conscience has been "seared" through past sin, can it ever be made tender again?

No foolproof mechanical method exists that will always cause us to properly interpret the urgings of the conscience. For each individual, the function of the conscience depends to some degree on background, maturity as a Christian, the amount of Scripture in the mind and life, and responses to the Bible and to the conscience in the past.

But if we understand biblical teaching about the conscience and the proper response to it, we will find it to be one of the key tools in discerning God's will in the difficult "gray" areas of our lives.

HOW GOD DIRECTS US

Although not everyone wants to *do* God's will, everyone does want to *know* it. People debate and question many ways in which God gives direction—such things as providential circumstances, unusual happenings, open and closed doors, dreams, prayers for evidences, "fleeces," and other devices. Some of these situations can be legitimate directions from God. But if they are used as isolated sources in determining God's will, they can be completely misleading.

God uses four basic means of giving us direction:

- the Bible (His Word);
- the Holy Spirit;
- counsel from godly people; and
- the conscience.

The Bible
God's Word provides the key source of direction for every Christian. Counsel, the leading of our conscience, and the Holy Spirit's guidance must not be contrary to the teaching of Scripture.

Scripture teaches and leads us by commands, principles, and examples. Therefore we must know what the Bible says and what it means, and apply this to our lives. "All Scripture is inspired by God and profitable for teaching, for reproof, for correction, for training in righteousness; that the man of God may be adequate, equipped for every good work" (2 Timothy 3:16-17). The Bible is the absolute guide for every area of life. Trying to find God's will without it is like trying to fly a complex airliner without a pilot's manual—risky, if not impossible.

THE HOLY SPIRIT

Incorporating the Holy Spirit in the search for direction is not a mystical or uncertain process. The Spirit of God uses the Word of God to speak to people today. "For to us God revealed them [the things He has prepared for us] through the Spirit; for the Spirit searches all things, even the depths of God. For who among men knows the thoughts of a man except the spirit of the man, which is in him? Even so the thoughts of God no one knows except the Spirit of God. Now we have received, not the spirit of the world, but the Spirit who is from God, that we might know the things freely given to us by God" (1 Corinthians 2:10-12). Before Jesus Christ returned to heaven He promised His disciples that He would send the Holy Spirit to live in them, to teach them truth, to give them discernment, and to encourage them in the life of righteousness. (A careful reading of John 14–16 will detail this work of the Holy Spirit in the life of every believer.)

How can we understand what the Bible says? The Spirit of God, who lives in every believer in Christ, gives understanding of the Scriptures. That is why it is vital for every Christian to be studying and reading the Bible, so the Holy Spirit can properly instruct us through God's Word.

COUNSEL FROM GODLY PEOPLE

God uses other believers to help us discover His will. No one can tell us what to do; we must accept personal responsibility for our actions. But a mature Christian friend can often see our situation or dilemma more objectively than we can, as Solomon indicated in the Proverbs:

> The way of a fool is right in his own eyes, but a wise man is he who listens to counsel. (12:15)

> Through presumption comes nothing but strife, but with those who receive counsel is wisdom. (13:10)

> Where there is no guidance, the people fall, but in abundance of counselors there is victory. (11:14)

One word of caution is needed here: In moral, ethical, and spiritual issues, do not rely on a nonbelieving friend for counsel. Even though they may be good people, they do not have a godly, spiritual, and biblical perspective. Scripture emphasizes this principle: "How blessed is the man who does not walk in the counsel of the wicked, nor stand in the path of sinners, nor sit in the seat of scoffers!" (Psalm 1:1).

Also, not every Christian gives godly counsel. We must use discernment in selecting a counselor, and know something of his or her life and walk with God. When we seek counsel from a mature believer—one who has personally experienced God's leading; who demonstrates a stable, holy way of life; and who uses the Bible in giving advice—we can be assured that his counsel will not run contrary to God's Word. As Hebrews says, "Remember those who led you, who spoke the word of God to you; and considering the outcome of their way of life, imitate their faith" (13:7).

THE CONSCIENCE

The conscience is mentioned often in Scripture. The apostle Paul stated, "I also do my best to maintain always a blameless conscience both before God and before men" (Acts 24:16). And describing unbelievers, he spoke of "their conscience bearing witness, and their thoughts alternately accusing or else defending them" (Romans 2:15).

God uses our conscience to give us direction. But what is a conscience? How does it function? How should we respond to its urgings?

FUNCTIONS AND CHARACTERISTICS OF THE CONSCIENCE

The English word *conscience* comes from the Latin word *conscientia*. The prefix *con* means "with" or "together."[2] The verb *scire*, from which the second part of the word is derived, means "to know."[3] Thus the word means "to know with" or "to know together." The Greek word used in the New Testament is *suneidesis*. Again it means "to know with," "to see together," or "to agree with."[4]

But we must ask, to know and to agree with what? To see together with whom?

With God—to agree with Him regarding right or wrong.

But could it not also mean to agree with our heritage, our teaching, our conditioning, our environment, and our culture? Yes, but God intends that the reference point— the point of comparison—for our lives should be His character and His standards. Frequently the conscience goes far beyond heritage, teaching, and environment. Something within man struggles against all his background and environment to declare that an act is right or wrong regardless of the standards that surround him.

Norwegian theologian O. Hallesby says, "Conscience is a consciousness of a holy, superhuman law." The conscience does not enforce obedience to itself, Hallesby says, but allows man to "freely and without compulsion follow that law which he through conscience recognizes as the law which he ought to follow."[5] The conscience thus provides a basis for making right decisions.

Hallesby also says conscience is *not* like instinct—the inner urge that compels animals to pursue a certain behavior—but that it is a knowledge, or consciousness.[6]

The eighteenth-century German philosopher Immanuel Kant said, "Two things fill the mind with ever increasing wonder and awe, the more often and the more intensely the mind of thought is drawn to them—the starry heavens above me and the moral law within me."[7]

The conscience is that part of every person which, willingly or unwillingly, responds to a universal moral law—in fact, to God's moral law. It communicates this awareness to the mind, forcing the mind to either obey or ignore the urging of conscience.

But instead of examining more human definitions, let us turn to the Bible to see how this mysterious conscience functions.

THE CONSCIENCE BEARS WITNESS

When comparing the Jewish Law of the Old Testament with the moral law within unbelievers, Paul said, "For when Gentiles who do not have the Law do instinctively the things of the Law, these, not having the Law, are a law to themselves, in that they show the work of the Law written in their hearts, *their conscience bearing witness,* and their thoughts alternately accusing or else defending them" (Romans 2:14-15, emphasis added). This passage gives significant insight into the conscience. Paul said there is an inner law which reflects God's Law and is "written in their hearts, their conscience bearing witness." The conscience "bears witness" between an outward action and the inner law. A witness is one who tells what he saw or heard, and the conscience is a witness of our actions and thoughts. The words *bearing witness* are in the present tense, and indicate that the conscience is active at all times.

Paul said later, "I am telling the truth in Christ, I am

not lying, my conscience bearing me witness in the Holy Spirit" (Romans 9:1). The witness of the conscience here relates Paul's action and the Holy Spirit (God). His conscience accurately and faithfully witnessed the rightness of his words and actions.

Your conscience is bearing witness of your actions right now. When you recall your actions of the past few days, what does your conscience say? It is trying to give you an accurate witness of how you measured up to God's standards.

THE CONSCIENCE ACCUSES OR EXCUSES

Notice also that Paul said the thoughts of unbelievers were "alternately *accusing or else defending* them" (Romans 2:15, emphasis added). When I spoke harshly to the produce manager, my conscience accused me of doing something wrong. Most people respond with anger or defensiveness when they are accused, so it is natural to rebel against the accusation of our conscience, as I did. This is highly uncomfortable, since the anger is directed against ourselves. And, still more frustrating, the anger has no effect on the opinion of our conscience. It continues to accuse.

On the other hand, our conscience may excuse or defend what we have done. Others may question our action, but our conscience will give us the peace of mind that our action was right.

THE CONSCIENCE JUDGES OUR ACTIONS

Paul reviewed his conduct among the Corinthians and declared that his conscience testified that he had conducted himself properly: "For our proud confidence is this, the testimony of our conscience, that in holiness and godly sincerity, not in fleshly wisdom but in the grace of God, we have conducted ourselves in the world, and especially toward you" (2 Corinthians 1:12).

Hallesby says the conscience cannot act, but only passes

judgment: "It compares our deeds or our words or our thoughts or our whole being with the moral law, with the will of God. And then [it] pronounces judgment, that is, decides whether we are in conformity or in conflict with the will of God."[8] Hallesby describes this judgment in the following four ways:[9]

First, he says, this judgment is final and unbiased. The conscience does not reconsider the evidence—it simply makes the final judgment. It is unbiased in that it takes the information given to it and pronounces the verdict. *It may not always be right,* but it is final in any given situation at any particular point in time.

Second, the conscience is irrefutable, absolute, and unappealable. Once having spoken, the conscience cannot be convinced, cajoled, or commanded to change its ruling. The conscience may grow stronger, or be seared, or turned more to God, and thus be altered later. But, right now, for this act, it is unappealable.

Third, the conscience is categorical. That is, it gives its judgment and supplies no reasons. It does not explain why it judges an action in a particular way, but says only that the action is right or wrong.

Fourth, the conscience is individual. One man's conscience will not judge the same way as another's. It speaks only to one individual, not to anyone else, and it is influenced by the many teachings and experiences unique to that person. This influence, of course, can be positive when the conscience is exposed to the higher law of God as revealed in the Bible.

We may add also that the conscience is *not* infallible. Conscience can be wrong. It can be perverted. It can be seared. And thus, it cannot be our only guide. "Let your conscience be your guide" is insufficient counsel.

Also, the conscience operates in the lives of both Christians and nonChristians. In the passage quoted earlier

(Romans 2:14-15), Paul said that the Gentiles (or unbelievers) were a law to themselves, and that this law was discerned by their conscience. The conscience is the God-given inner sense in every human. Hallesby says it is *the irreplaceable thing* in human life. It is that which makes us human beings."[10]

The conscience convicts even when an act does not appear to be morally wrong. When King David had a census taken in Israel, his action was not in itself morally wrong. Yet, "David's heart [conscience] troubled him after he had numbered the people. So David said to the Lord, 'I have sinned greatly in what I have done'" (2 Samuel 24:10). Why was his action wrong? Perhaps because God did not want him to depend on numbers of soldiers, but on Him. David's motive may have been his sin, and God spoke through David's conscience. Though an action may seem entirely permissible, both legally and morally, God may force our conscience to instruct us not to do it.

We all know we possess a conscience. It constantly speaks by condemning us for wrong deeds or commending us for right actions. We all long to have a clear conscience before God and men. Even the world recognizes the value of a clear conscience. Adam Smith wrote: "What can be added to the happiness of a man who is healthy, who is out of debt, and who has a clear conscience?"[11]

Notes

1. Reprinted by permission of the *Chicago Tribune*-New York News Syndicate.
2. *Webster's New Collegiate Dictionary* (Springfield, Mass.: G. and C. Merriam Company, 1974), p. 223 (*con-*).
3. *Webster's New Collegiate Dictionary*, p. 240 (*conscience*).
4. W. E. Vine, *An Expository Dictionary of New Testament Words* (London: Oliphants, Ltd., 1940), vol. I, p. 228.
5. Reprinted from *Conscience*, by O. Hallesby, ©1933, 1961, by permission of Augsburg Publishing House, p. 14.
6. Hallesby, *Conscience*, p. 13.
7. Immanuel Kant, *Critique of Pure Reason*, 1781.

8. Hallesby, *Conscience*, p. 29.
9. Hallesby, *Conscience*, pp. 29-30.
10. Hallesby, *Conscience*, p. 140.
11. Adam Smith, *The Theory of Moral Sentiments*, 1853, as quoted in *Time*, 14 July 1975, p. 55.

Chapter Three

HOW TO USE AND RESPOND TO YOUR CONSCIENCE

———————— ∽ ————————

M y wife and I had gone away for a two-day holiday and were relaxing in a motel. One morning I sat by the pool reading a book on Christian personal ethics and studying a chapter that discussed the conscience. Nearby I noticed two men with cameras. One of the men approached me and asked if I would mind if they included me in their pictures. I said that would be no problem and to go ahead. He then mentioned that some girls were changing into bathing suits and would soon join us. Although I was puzzled, it seemed normal, since we were at a swimming pool.

A short while later three young women came to the pool. The photographer arranged them around me as I sat in a chair, and snapped some pictures. I felt a bit uncomfortable even though nothing improper took place. The photographer then directed the women to various places around the pool and took more shots of them.

One of the girls noticed that I was reading a Christian book and asked, "Are you a Christian?" When I responded affirmatively, she said she was a Christian too, and after a pause asked, "Doesn't your wife mind you having your picture taken with someone else?"

"No, she's quite secure," I answered, mentioning that she was in our room and was aware that the pictures were being taken. "By the way," I asked her, "what are these pictures for?"

"Oh, they're for an advertising brochure for the motel," she answered.

The photography session ended and I returned to the room. As I described the situation to Mary, doubt crept into my mind. What if someone should see those pictures in the brochure, recognize me, and misinterpret the circumstances? I was innocent, but the situation disturbed my conscience. Before long I became uneasy. I wondered if I had been wrong in permitting the pictures to be taken.

Later that morning I went to the office to pay our bill, and the motel sales manager was there. I asked him what the pictures were for, and he confirmed that they would be used in an advertising brochure. He also said the photographs were taken with a wide-angle lens, and that the people would appear very small and probably would not be recognizable.

Well, I thought, *it's all right.*

But as I carried our baggage from the motel room, my conscience still bothered me. I felt concerned about how it might affect The Navigators and my Christian testimony if I were recognized. I located the sales manager again and asked him not to use my picture. I apologized for allowing the photographs to be taken, and explained that I was in a Christian organization and that the photographs could be misinterpreted. To my surprise he said he certainly understood, and he apologized for not telling me what the pictures were for. He said the arrangements had been very last-minute and unplanned.

This circumstance illustrates an action that in itself was not wrong, yet my conscience urged me to reverse my decision. When I finally changed the circumstances, peace was restored.

Now perhaps I was too sensitive. Or maybe I wasn't sensitive enough, and my conscience tried to speak to me before the pictures were taken but I wouldn't listen. Regardless, my conscience kept prodding me until I obeyed, even though no ethical wrong existed. How should we respond to urgings like this?

When Conscience Functions

The conscience functions at all times, but its strength and its ability to influence us varies. At times it speaks faintly and at times it rages.

Before a contemplated action is begun, the conscience attempts to communicate whether the action would be right or wrong. At this point the battle is in the mind. The conscience wrestles with a confusion of proposals, reasons, impulses, and motives. How strongly it speaks is much influenced by information that has been fed to our mind and by what we have been thinking about most.

This is the point at which the battle for purity, morality, and honesty must be fought and won. What is harbored in the mind will soon become an action when the opportunity presents itself, so the conscience needs an opportunity to speak before an action takes place.

A few years ago a young man who had been a believer in Christ only a short time was sent to Asia for a three-month military assignment. Opportunities for sin and immorality surrounded him. When he returned he said, "I'm so glad I studied the Bible before I went. When you're 10,000 miles from home, it's easy to think you're 10,000 miles from God. But the Scriptures and my conscience were my source of strength in resisting temptation."

During an action the conscience is usually at its weakest level of influence. We become so involved in what we are doing that we are insensitive to the cries of conscience. We may hear it, but rush forward with the action while making some weak rationalization in our minds. Once an act of wrong has begun, stopping it is extremely difficult. Momentum, desire, and the intensity of the moment seem to overrule any reversal. But it can be done. At this point the will must overcome the desire. We cannot discount our conscience even when involved in the worst of acts. It is better to obey now than later.

The conscience speaks loudest *after* an act has been completed, as it pronounces judgment on the act. Our conscience urges us to make restitution for the action. We can respond to this in various ways. After David's conscience struck him when he numbered Israel, he confessed and repented of what he had done (2 Samuel 24:10). Adam and Eve, on the other hand, hid from God after disobeying Him (Genesis 3:7-8).

The desire to escape results naturally when we sin and our conscience speaks. We shun God's presence until we have obeyed the urgings of our conscience. Maintaining fellowship with God is closely related to keeping a clear conscience.

What the Conscience Judges

The conscience speaks about much more than our actions. It also judges our *words*—what we say and how we say it. We are judged according to the truthfulness, love, and kindness expressed through our communications to others. We may quickly experience reproach from our conscience if we speak harshly, untruthfully, bitterly, or angrily.

The conscience also judges our *thoughts*. We often suppress our conscience on this point since no visible action has yet occurred, and our thoughts are often confused and fleeting. But the conscience works primarily on recurring, persistent thoughts and thought patterns that are neither temporary nor harmless. They can soon become dominant thought patterns that quickly result in wrong actions. The conscience warns us when these thoughts begin.

Our *attitudes* are also judged by the conscience. Attitudes are our inner feelings or opinions about things. We harbor attitudes of love, hate, sympathy, bitterness, anger, unconcern, and many others. They can be healthy or unhealthy. Attitudes are one level below our conscious thoughts, but conscience has ready access to this level.

Finally, the conscience also judges our *motives*. Whereas our attitudes reside within us and may not result in action, motives are the direct, underlying reasons why we take particular actions.

A right motive may produce either a proper or improper action. For example, if a parent is correcting a child, his motive should be to prepare the child to be a godly person and a contributing citizen in society. The parent can do this by love, counsel, and discipline, which are proper biblical actions. But prompted by the same motive, a parent can scold, belittle, ridicule, and make unreasonable demands—improper actions that are, incidentally, unproductive.

THE KINDS OF CONSCIENCE

Ron was a student in a prominent university. Through the witness and influence of some believers on campus he accepted Christ into his life. He began to change radically as he grew spiritually: He stopped cursing, he repaired a broken relationship with his father, he studied the Bible, and he shared his new faith with his friends. However, he was still living with his girlfriend. His new Christian friends were concerned about this but said nothing. Finally, another Christian spoke to him and showed him several Scripture passages that told him his action was wrong. Ron was amazed, and responded immediately by moving out. He simply had not known that his actions were wrong. In the current campus society, his situation was so normal as to appear right. Without previous knowledge of scriptural teachings in this area, he had no information for his conscience to draw upon.

Ron's situation is evidence of the various states our conscience can hold. Scripture has a great deal to say about these different states.

A Good Conscience

While standing before his accusers, Paul said, "I have lived my life with a perfectly good conscience before God" (Acts 23:1). This does not mean Paul never sinned or violated his conscience, but that when his conscience spoke he responded promptly and properly. He said his good conscience was "before God," indicating that God was the basis of his judgment and the reference point for his conscience.

Paul commanded Timothy to keep "faith and a good conscience, which some have rejected and suffered shipwreck in regard to their faith" (1 Timothy 1:19). Rejecting a good conscience has a devastating effect on our faith. (See also 1 Timothy 3:8-9.) Susanna Wesley wrote these penetrating words plainly describing the threats to a good conscience: "Whatever weakens your reason, impairs the tenderness of your conscience, or obscures your sense of God or takes off the relish of spiritual things; whatever increases the authority of your body over your mind, that thing to you is sin."[1]

An Evil Conscience

God's Word also speaks of an evil conscience. The writer to the Hebrews said, "Let us draw near with a sincere heart in full assurance of faith, having our hearts sprinkled clean from an evil conscience and our bodies washed with pure water" (10:22). The Bible does not precisely define an "evil conscience," but we can learn more about it from the context of this verse. The writer says earlier that the blood of

Christ will "cleanse your conscience from dead works" (9:14). We can conclude that an evil conscience is one that bears the knowledge of sins—"dead works"—that have not been confessed and cleansed. The Greek word used for evil in Hebrews 10:22 is *poneros*, which "denotes evil that causes labor, pain, sorrow."[2]

The evil conscience is an uncleansed conscience, not a conscience that prompts us to do evil things. As a result of unconfessed sin, the person with an evil conscience becomes more susceptible to sin and less sensitive to what is good.

A Seared Conscience

In his first letter to Timothy, Paul spoke of hypocritical liars who were "seared in their own conscience as with a branding iron," and who caused others to "fall away from the faith, paying attention to deceitful spirits and doctrines of demons" (4:1-2). *The Living Bible* paraphrases this passage describing the seared conscience: "These teachers will tell lies with straight faces and do it so often that their consciences won't even bother them." In another letter he described unbelievers as "being darkened in their understanding, excluded from the life of God, because of the ignorance that is in them, because of the hardness of their heart; and they, having become callous, have given themselves over to sensuality, for the practice of every kind of impurity with greediness" (Ephesians 4:18-19).

These passages describe perfectly those whose conscience has been made insensitive. They are hypocritical and callous. Their conscience has been branded. Imagine a hot branding iron touching your skin. First you feel terrible pain, but then numbness. When the wound later heals, the scar has no functioning nerve endings to produce feeling.

Or touch a well-developed callous on your hand—you can't even feel a tickle. A seared conscience is like that. Although at one time deeply sensitive, it was burned and destroyed by the toleration of sin and is now insensitive. The seared conscience finally becomes silent when the same sin is committed repeatedly.

Oswald Chambers wrote this about the seared conscience:

Conscience is the eye of the soul recording what it looks at, but if what Ruskin calls the "innocence of the eye" is lost, then the recording conscience may be distorted. If I continually twist the organ of my soul's recording, it will become perverted. If I do a wrong thing often enough, I cease to realise the wrong in it. A bad man can be perfectly happy in his badness. That is what a seared conscience means.[3]

Can a seared conscience be made sensitive again? Fortunately, the conscience is not like our skin. The conscience can experience healing and restoration. If the conscience has lost its sensitivity, it can be retrained by the Word of God.

But until the conscience has become reliable again, actions must be based on a direct response to the teachings of Scripture instead of the advice of the conscience. This regeneration process must go on until the urgings of conscience begin to agree consistently with Scripture in the areas where it has been seared. This could take quite a long time.

It is possible for the conscience to be seared and unreliable in one area and reliable in another—with some limitations. For example, your conscience may goad you about lying, yet be completely insensitive to sexual sin. But harboring sin in one area of your life does spill over into other areas. A conscience seared in one area will eventually be weakened in all areas.

The conscience may function fairly strongly according to a person's background and past teaching, rather than being based directly on Scripture. Many nonbelievers live a moral life consistent with much of the Bible without basing their actions on its teachings.

A WEAK CONSCIENCE

The conscience can be weak in one of two ways—being either immature or oversensitive. Speaking of the immature conscience, Paul told the Corinthians, "Take care lest this liberty of yours somehow become a stumbling block to the weak. For if someone sees you, who have knowledge, dining in an idol's temple, will not his conscience, if he is weak, be strengthened to eat things sacrificed to idols? For through your knowledge he who is weak is ruined, the brother for whose sake Christ died. And thus, by sinning against the brethren and wounding their conscience when it is weak, you sin against Christ" (1 Corinthians 8:9-12).

The issue here is that the believer with a weak conscience may be led into sin by imitating or misinterpreting the actions of another believer. A new believer retains many cultural and religious ideas from his nonChristian past. Confusion often results when he tries to determine what it means to live as a Christian. He needs to develop his conscience by studying and applying Scripture.

J. Oswald Sanders helps us understand the oversensitive conscience. He writes, "Many sensitive Christians have limped through life because of a morbid and weak conscience whose condemning voice allowed them no respite. Their very sincerity and desire to do the will of God only accentuated the problem and caused them to live in a state of perpetual self-accusation."[4]

Take Chuck's example. He was walking down a sidewalk when he saw a broken bottle. He passed by, but felt a pang of conscience. *What if someone comes along, falls, and cuts himself?* he thought. *Then it would be my fault because I saw it and didn't pick it up.* He walked on, stopped, struggled with his conscience, walked on—but finally gave in and came back and picked up the bottle.

Was there anything wrong with picking up the bottle? No. Was it a thoughtful act? Yes. But Chuck experienced this predicament dozens of times a day. Nails, a piece of wood, a slick spot on the floor, and countless other minor things would distract and trouble his conscience. His conscientiousness paralyzed him. He had to correct every problem or suffer guilt.

Let us look at another example. In a passing remark, Judy commented to Connie that she had tried to call her six times the day before, and also that she had spent an hour on the phone with a mutual friend. After she left Connie, her conscience began to bother her. Was it six times or just four? Was it really an hour or just fifty minutes? Did it really matter? It did to her. Soon she was paralyzed, thinking she had lied. She called Connie and asked her forgiveness.

Both Judy and Chuck were prisoners of a weak, oversensitive conscience. Chuck needed to realize that he cannot replace God in protecting the population of his city. Certainly he should be concerned and correct obvious hazards, but agonizing over small things prevented him from normal functioning. Judy needed to discern between deliberate lying and honest mistakes.

The root problem of an oversensitive conscience is legalism. It is living in fear of the letter of an unwritten law, and harboring an underlying apprehension that if the exact details of the law are not met, the relationship with God will be hindered or broken or another person will be hurt. In extreme cases this problem can lead to a nervous breakdown.

Some basic steps for altering an overly sensitive conscience are:

1. Clearly understand from Scripture that our standing with God is based on His grace and not works (Romans 5:1, Ephesians 2:8-9).

2. Study Scripture passages on the sovereignty of God as it relates to you and others.
3. Ask God to develop your conscience according to His standards.
4. Refuse the urgings of your conscience in a sensitive area unless you can see that they directly conform to a moral command in Scripture.
5. If the problem persists, seek help from a mature, trusted believer or a biblically based counselor. Talking openly about the various issues can confirm and clarify your thinking.

The apostle John wrote, "This then is how we know that we belong to the truth, and how we set our hearts at rest in His presence whenever our hearts condemn us. For God is greater than our hearts, and He knows everything" (1 John 3:19-20, NIV).

It is well to note, however, that many more people are inclined to ignore and resist the work of the conscience than to have an oversensitive conscience.

A DEFILED CONSCIENCE

If we continually ignore the leading of the Word *and* conscience, the conscience becomes defiled or corrupted. "To the pure, all things are pure" Paul wrote, "but to those who are defiled and unbelieving, nothing is pure, but both their mind and their conscience are defiled" (Titus 1:15). In this state, the conscience loses its ability to discern right and wrong—and, in fact, may approve what is corrupt. The word *defiled* connotes a mixing of the pure and impure.

Obviously, the defiled conscience and the seared conscience are similar. The difference is that the seared conscience is totally insensitive, whereas the defiled conscience is misguided by a combination of right and wrong. (See also 1 Corinthians 8:7.)

HOW TO FOLLOW YOUR CONSCIENCE

We have to this point detected several problems in knowing when to follow your conscience:

- The conscience can be insensitive or seared, and therefore incapable of giving direction.
- It can be too tender or weak, and therefore unreliable.
- It is not an absolute authority, since it is conditioned by background and teaching.
- It is inadequate when used alone and must be supplemented with the influence of God's Word, the Holy Spirit, and godly counsel.

RESPONDING PROPERLY TO THE CONSCIENCE

Because the conscience is inadequate by itself, we must take certain steps to verify its urgings. The correct pattern for this process is pictured in figure 3.1.

1. First we commit an act, say a word, think a thought, or harbor an attitude, or else we simply contemplate one of these actions.

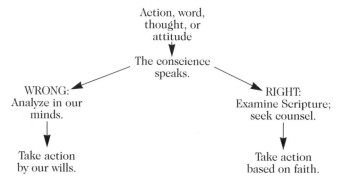

Figure 3.1
Responding to the Conscience

2. The conscience then speaks, giving its judgment regarding the rightness or wrongness of the situation.

3. At this point we may be tempted to analyze the situation with our minds and take action by our wills. This is the wrong approach. The next step *must* be to examine Scripture to see what it says about the issue. Even when the Bible does not speak directly about it, we need to be reading and studying Scripture regularly so the Holy Spirit can use it to direct us.

4. We should seek counsel from a godly friend if we do not have clear direction at this point.

5. Finally, we must act on the basis of faith. As Paul wrote, "Whatever is not from faith is sin" (Romans 14:23).

To respond correctly to what our conscience says, we may need to *make restitution* to someone for what we have done, or *confess* something — first to God, then to others. Or we may need to *stop or start doing something*—such as controlling our tongue or being more helpful in the home. We may need to *change an attitude* about another person or situation, or *forgive* someone for something they have done to us, even if they have not asked for forgiveness. In any case, to have a clear conscience before God and man (Acts 24:16) we must do whatever is necessary.

HOW TO TRAIN AND STRENGTHEN YOUR CONSCIENCE

All the understanding and knowledge about the conscience will be fruitless if it is not changed into a sensitive tool in God's hand. How can the conscience be trained, changed, or developed? Several keys are:

Have a Christian Conscience

The only way to have a Christian conscience is to *be* a Christian. Many people are deeply moral and even intensely religious, but are not Christians in the biblical sense. Perhaps the struggles you are having in the area of conscience are a means God is using to help you make a positive, personal commitment to Him.

The process of becoming a Christian is simple and is explained in Scripture. First, recognize and admit that you are sinful (Romans 3:23) and that your sin has separated you from God.

Second, recognize that Jesus Christ died for you and your sin, and that He offers you the free gift of eternal life (Romans 5:8, John 3:16).

Third, simply ask Christ to be your Lord and Savior and to give you eternal life (John 1:12, 5:24).[5]

When you believe in Christ your conscience has two new sources of input — the Holy Spirit and the Bible. They are vital to make your conscience the instrument God intended.

Regular Intake of God's Word

Many people take in Scripture only when they hear someone preach. Though sermons are a good start, they are inadequate for the strong development of conscience. Every Christian needs to read God's Word daily. We must set aside a time each day to read the Bible and to pray over what we read. Ten or fifteen minutes of daily prayer and Bible reading will be life-changing.[6]

When we regularly spend time with God in His Word, we are often surprised how our conscience specifically guides us in the "gray" areas of life.

Obedience

Another key to developing conscience is to obey the Word of God and the conscience. We begin by obeying in obvious

CHECKOUT SLIP
NEW LONDON PUBLIC
LIBRARY
PHONE: 419-929-3981

User ID:
24407000048636

Title: The miracle worker
[DVD]
Item ID:
33064009476349
Date due: 6/3/2016,23:
59

Title: Honesty, morality, &
conscience
Item ID:
32487005029435
Date due: 6/17/2016,23:
59

www.
newlondonpubliclibrary.
org

areas of life where God has clearly been trying to speak (such as an area of sin, our lack of fellowship with other Christians, our lack of developing relationships with non-believers, or poor personal relationships in our family). Then we must consistently follow the urging of the conscience.

Scripture Memory

Memorizing portions of Scripture gives the Holy Spirit a tool to use in training the conscience. "How can a young man keep his way pure? By keeping it according to Thy word," the psalmist wrote. "Thy word I have treasured in my heart, that I may not sin against Thee" (Psalm 119:9,11). Occupying our minds with Scripture will have a profound effect on the sensitivity of the conscience.

We must train our conscience to respond properly. It will not happen automatically. We must determine to do it and diligently pursue it. Then we can have the same conviction as Martin Luther, who answered his accusers, "My conscience is bound in the Word of God. I cannot and will not recant anything, since it is unsafe and dangerous to act against conscience. Here I stand. I cannot do otherwise."[7]

Notes
1. This quote is attributed to Susanna Wesley. Source unknown.
2. W. E. Vine, *An Expository Dictionary of New Testament Words*, vol. II, p. 50.
3. Oswald Chambers, *Our Brilliant Heritage*, as quoted in *Oswald Chambers: The Best from All His Books*, Harry Verploegh, ed. (Nashville: Oliver Nelson, 1987), p. 65.
4. J. Oswald Sanders, *A Spiritual Clinic* (Chicago: Moody, 1958), p. 57.
5. For further study on becoming a Christian, see *How to Be Born Again* by Billy Graham (Waco, Tex.: Word Books, 1977) and *Becoming a Christian* by John R. W. Stott (Downers Grove, Ill.: Inter-Varsity, 1950).
6. For further help in establishing a daily devotional time, see the pamphlet *Seven Minutes with God*, published by NavPress and available at Christian bookstores.
7. As quoted by O. Hallesby, *Conscience*, p. 36.

Chapter Four

HONESTY —
THE BIBLICAL MANDATE

———————— ❧ ————————

A salesman knocked on the door of a run-down and obviously poor home. The mother in the home told her little boy to tell the salesman she could not come to the door because she was in the bathtub. The little boy went to the door and said, "We ain't got no bathtub, but Mom told me to tell you she's in it."

This is a refreshing story—a joke, yes, but also a commentary on our view of honesty. The constant strain between expediency and honesty causes most of us, at some time, to compromise our standards and violate our consciences.

Dishonesty has become a way of life in our society— candy bar wrappers twice the size of the candy; plastic toys that have no chance of surviving a few hours of play; advertisements that ignore a product's faults and exaggerate its quality; cheating on automobile repairs; cheating in the classroom; and infidelity in marriage. These and other practices condition us to be suspicious of everyone and to live on the edge of dishonesty ourselves.

But what is true honesty? Is it simply *not* cheating, stealing, or lying? How do we set standards for living honestly? Can anyone ever be totally honest?

Some equate honesty with the law. Anything that is permissible within the written law of the land is honest. If the law does not specify right and wrong about an action, then that action is right. As a result, thousands of volumes of detailed laws have been written to control everything from premeditated murder to parking violations.

Some view honesty as a matter of individual conscience. They obey the written law only because of the attached penalties. The real law, they say, is within. There is no real wrong—anything is lawful unless it violates the conscience.

To others, honesty is a reflection of the golden rule: "Just as you want men to treat you, treat them in the same way" (Luke 6:31). This, too, involves a subjective judgment. No fixed standards exist.

Others experience honesty as a self-imposed legalism that goes far beyond either the written law of society or the Bible. Honesty then becomes a fabricated set of rules to cover every action and word.

Still others say the practice of honesty depends on the situation. Does it feel right? What seems right in one situation may be wrong in another. Consequently, no real standards exist.

Does the Bible give absolute standards of honesty? Can we turn to a passage of Scripture for a clear answer to every dilemma of honesty? Not necessarily. The Bible does give many definite guidelines and specific commands on various aspects of honesty. But primarily the Scriptures present general principles of conduct. The Holy Spirit can use these to cause our consciences to discern what is honest and right.

Honesty, as described in the Bible, is much broader than simply abstaining from lying. For instance, while writing about his commitment to the honest administration of money given for a relief fund, Paul said, "For we have regard for what is *honorable* not only in the sight of the Lord, but also in the sight of men" (2 Corinthians 8:21, emphasis added). Honesty involves an upright way of life and proper thought patterns that result in an honorable lifestyle.

An honest lifestyle develops from diligent effort and prayer. "Pray for us," the writer to the Hebrews said, "for we are sure that we have a good conscience, desiring to conduct ourselves honorably in all things" (13:18). Honesty must encompass our entire manner of life as well as specific details of truthfulness, for it is possible to be scrupulously honest in one area of life and flagrantly dishonest in another.

Let us look now at the many facets of honesty and dishonesty.

TRUTH

Shortly before delivering Him up to be crucified, Pilate asked Jesus, "What is truth?" (John 18:38). This is an age-old question. Truth obviously comprises an integral part of honesty. Being honest is certainly being truthful.

There are many categories of truth. *Scientific truth* can be verified by accepted scientific procedures. This truth generally relates to physical facts such as a particular type of metal, the identification of a tree, or the working of an automobile engine. Scientific truth should not be confused with scientific theories, such as biological evolution or the structure of the atom.

When a person expresses his religious beliefs he describes *doctrinal truth* based on an interpretation of Scripture. Most believers agree with such fundamental doctrines as the deity of Christ, the authority of Scripture, and salvation in Jesus Christ. But many other issues receive various interpretations—baptism, church government, worship style, and prophecy. Disagreement on doctrinal truth does not comprise lying or dishonesty, unless Scripture is grossly misused, as it is in many cults.

Another kind of truth is that embodied in *Jesus Christ*

and the Word of God. Jesus said, "I am the way, and the truth, and the life; no one comes to the Father, but through Me" (John 14:6). Jesus claimed to be the embodiment of God's truth. In Scripture He is Himself called the Word (John 1:14). Jesus prayed, "Thy Word is truth" (John 17:17). In this sense, God—the source of all truth—has revealed this truth through Christ and in Scripture. If Christ and the Bible are truth, we can confidently base a definition of personal honesty and truthfulness on the Scripture.

The most common use of the word truth is as *facts*. Presenting accurate facts is the opposite of lying. If someone asks you what time you arrived at work and you answer, "7:52," you have related a clear fact that can be proven or disproven.

Paul said, "I am telling the truth in Christ, I am not lying, my conscience bearing me witness in the Holy Spirit" (Romans 9:1). Notice the relationship he presented of truth, not lying, conscience, and the Holy Spirit. Paul called both his conscience and the Holy Spirit as witnesses that he was telling the truth.

Lying

In Scripture God condemns lying in any form. "A lying tongue" and "a false witness who utters lies" are listed as things that are abominations to Him (Proverbs 6:16-19).

But lying happens so easily, especially when speaking the truth counters what we want. We find it easy to shade the truth—changing it just enough to suit our desires. We fall into the habit of lying to God, lying to friends, lying to coworkers—and even lying to ourselves.

An old 1962 Volkswagen "bug" had been a part of our family since it was new. When I sold it recently, I knew all of its good and bad points. How much should I tell a prospective buyer? Only what he asked? All I knew? I concluded that I needed to tell all I knew. What a sales pitch!

"The horn needs to be fixed. . . . You will need to get the brake pads replaced. . . . The backup lights do not work. . . . The wiper motor may be burned out." But I was able to include some good points also: It had a newly rebuilt engine, and the front end had been recently repaired. As I mentioned all this, the buyer gave me a squinty-eyed, quizzical look, obviously thinking, *And what else is wrong that he hasn't told me about?*

Well, the car sold to that first man who came to look at it. As I went to the Clerk's Office to complete the bill of sale, the buyer took me aside and whispered, "Put down that I paid you $300 for the car." But he had paid $500! I said, "I really would not feel right doing that since I am a Christian and it would be wrong." He said, "Well, I'm a Christian, too. I just hate to pay taxes when I don't have to." No one enjoys conflict, and I did want to please this man. Inwardly, I was tempted to agree with him—all for a six-dollar tax. But I didn't. He was disgusted. I'm sure he didn't tell me all he was thinking. But my conscience remained clear. I did not witness to him in a complete way, but perhaps at a later time he will associate honesty as a mark of a Christian. I hope our encounter will stay in his mind and provide an opportunity for the Holy Spirit to convict him later.

One of the key elements in a good relationship is truth, as we are told in Scripture: "Do not lie to one another, since you laid aside the old self with its evil practices" (Colossians 3:9). "Therefore, laying aside falsehood, speak truth, each one of you, with his neighbor, for we are members of one another" (Ephesians 4:25).

Lies destroy trust, and once trust is gone, a relationship is difficult to restore. Yet the habit of lying can develop so subtly that it goes unnoticed. We begin by lying about "small" things that "don't matter." Then we develop a pattern. Soon valuable credibility and friendships are lost.

SLANDER

Slander is a malicious form of lying. It is defined as "the utterance of false charges or misrepresentations which defame and damage another's reputation."[1]

God's Word speaks forcefully about slander: "Whoever secretly slanders his neighbor, him will I destroy" (Psalm 101:5). We read that the person who abides with God "does not slander with his tongue, nor does evil to his neighbor" (Psalm 15:3). Paul describes people in the last days as, among many other things, "malicious gossips" (2 Timothy 3:3). But Christians are commanded to "let all bitterness and wrath and anger and clamor and slander be put away" (Ephesians 4:31).

God hates slander. He will not approve the Christian who practices it. Yet, how quickly we relay questionable information about others. Second- and third-hand information becomes dangerous in the mind of one who tends to gossip. How often do we hear a person saying in a confidential tone, "Just so you can pray about it, I thought you would want to know about John . . ."? Or how many times have we heard something about someone and believed it without knowing if it was true?

Technically, slander is the communication of a lie about someone else. Even when the things we say are true, they can malign someone when we communicate them out of context or by not giving other truths at the same time. For example, we might say, "Did you know that Joyce left her husband for two weeks?" and not add, "to go help her sister when she was ill." Or we could say, "Have you heard that John refused to teach in our Sunday school?" without explaining that it was because he expected his company to transfer him in the next six months.

We need to guard our lips and minds. Slander can happen even unintentionally. "Let no unwholesome word proceed from your mouth," we are told, "but only such a word as is good for edification according to the need of the moment, that it may give grace to those who hear" (Ephesians 4:29).

DECEIT

To *deceive* means "to cause to accept as true or valid what is false or invalid."[2] It means to delude, mislead, or beguile. David reflected God's view of deceit when he said, "He who practices deceit shall not dwell within my house; he who speaks falsehood shall not maintain his position before me" (Psalm 101:7). David also said that a wicked man's words "are wickedness and deceit; he has ceased to be wise and to do good" (Psalm 36:3).

In the New Testament we are told, "See to it that no one takes you captive through philosophy and empty deception" (Colossians 2:8), but instead to put aside "all guile and hypocrisy and envy and all slander" (1 Peter 2:1). Peter also said, "Let him who means to love life and see good days refrain his tongue from evil and his lips from speaking guile" (1 Peter 3:10).

We practice deceit when we lead someone to believe a lie, even though we may be speaking true words. Referring back to my 1962 Volkswagen, I could have deceived a buyer by not honestly explaining the faults of the car. I could also have openly lied to deceive him, but generally we deceive in more subtle ways. We try to cover problems in our spiritual lives and personal relationships by making people think all is well. In our work we can deceive our employers by looking busy instead of really being productive, by filling out time reports that are not fully true, and by doing substandard work. When we tell about past sports accomplishments, our job activities and promotions, or personal relationships, we may try to paint a picture of ourselves that is exaggerated and false. In fact, we even begin to deceive ourselves, which is the most dangerous of deceits. Jeremiah said, "The heart is more deceitful than all else and is desperately sick; who can understand it?" (Jeremiah 17:9). The apostle James said, "If any one thinks himself to be religious, and yet does not bridle his tongue but deceives his own heart, this man's religion is worthless" (James 1:26). We can deceive our own hearts and believe our own lies about ourselves.

We can deceive others unknowingly. We may be unaware that certain information we have is confidential, and we may inadvertently share too much of it. But we must especially be concerned with deceit that is calculated, and based on wrong motives. When we know what we are doing and proceed even though our conscience or the Word points out to us that we are deceiving, we are blatantly sinning.

The story of Ananias and Sapphira (Acts 5:1-11) presents a vivid biblical example of an attempt to deceive. This couple sold a piece of property and kept part of the money for themselves, bringing the balance to the apostles as a gift. They did not sin in keeping part of the money, but rather by leading others to believe they had given everything. God rejected this attempt to deceive Him, and both Ananias and Sapphira quickly died.

CHEATING

Cheating is a clear form of dishonesty. Students cheat on exams, workers cheat on their employers' time, and citizens cheat on income taxes.

The Bible speaks to this topic. Because of its complexity, the subject will be examined more fully in chapters 6 and 8.

SILENCE

Many times silence is as dishonest as a spoken lie. God allows no fifth amendment. When we fail to communicate and others are misled by our silence, we have dealt dishonestly. When someone "knows the right thing to do, and does not do it, to him it is sin" (James 4:17).

Ezekiel also gave God's view of this principle: "If the watchman sees the sword coming and does not blow the trumpet, and the people are not warned, and a sword comes and takes a person from them, he is taken away in his iniquity; but his blood I will require from the watchman's hand" (Ezekiel 33:6). God said the watchman who saw the enemy but failed to warn the people would be held accountable.

Many times we know we should speak or warn someone, but we keep silent because of fear or a desire to avoid conflict. When we hear others gossip and slander, is it right to keep silent rather than tell the truth, or should we defend the person being slandered? In our work do we speak up for what is right, or just "hope" we won't have to be part of the dishonesty? Our silence can give assent to sin and dishonesty.

We need to be bold and to speak the truth regardless of the consequences. Peter and John said, "We cannot stop speaking what we have seen and heard" (Acts 4:20).

Silence can be sin.

INTEGRITY

Another aspect of honesty is integrity. Integrity is a wholesome or moral completeness, and is characteristic of a person whose life reflects the life of Jesus Christ. Integrity demonstrates the inner person—the motive behind the act. Solomon wrote, "A righteous man who walks in his integrity—how blessed are his sons after him" (Proverbs 20:7), and "Better is a poor man who walks in his integrity than he who is perverse in speech and is a fool" (Proverbs 19:1).

The psalmist wrote that David, as the leader of Israel, "shepherded them according to the integrity of his heart" (Psalm 78:72).

Integrity encompasses all of what we do and are—speech, motives, and actions. A mature Christian walks in integrity, inwardly and outwardly.

Obviously, honesty is more complex than simply not steal-ing money or not telling a bold lie. Honesty involves our deepest motives and encompasses every area of private and public life. It includes truth in every sense, and integrity in the inner person. Honesty demands putting aside lying, cheating, slander, and deceit—and, at times, even silence.

But simply defining and describing honesty is not the same as honest action. How can we apply this knowledge to daily living without becoming paranoid legalists who are unable to function for fear of being dishonest? The following chapters examine honesty in specific problem areas of life.

Notes
1. *Webster's New Collegiate Dictionary*, p. 1090.
2. *Webster's New Collegiate Dictionary*, p. 293.

Chapter Five

THE PROBLEM
OF PEER PRESSURE

———————— ❧ ————————

In college he grew a beard, wore overalls and dirty T-shirts, and "did" drugs. Then he graduated, shaved his beard, bought a new blue suit, and joined the corporate treadmill. He married, had two children, joined the right clubs, and bought a home in the suburbs. He sold his soul to the company.

Then his wife left him. He divorced her, became a playboy, and then remarried. He was promoted by his company. He cheated on taxes, his travel reports, and his wife.

He did none of these because he deeply wanted to or thought he should. Rather, they were the "right" things to do. They were acceptable. Everybody was doing them.

Yes, he was very, very successful—and very, very unhappy. Life had become a masquerade. By now he hardly knew who he was. Come to think of it, he was a little bit of everybody. Although fiercely claiming independence, he actually would do nothing that might endanger his standing with his peers.

He might well describe himself as American newspaper editor Emile Henry Gauvreau did, as being "part of that strange race of people aptly described as spending their lives doing things they detest to make money they don't want to buy things they don't need to impress people they dislike."[1]

The influence of people on people is a powerful force, affecting everyone. Only the power of God and the innate drive for physical survival outrank it. A reasoning mind can become powerless in the face of this pressure. Even the most committed individualist conforms in some ways to the lifestyle of others.

This influence is stronger than any of us would like to admit. We want to act individually and independently, but in reality we conform much of our life to those around us.

The pressure we face from others is one of the greatest barriers to making proper ethical decisions. Our study of honesty and conscience will fade into obscurity unless we know how to face this pressure. We need to understand its source, as well as how to overcome it.

Not all pressure from others is wrong. Pressure from some people can keep us from sin. One of the central concepts of fellowship among believers is our influence for good on each other. This peer pressure can restrain our tendency toward evil, and encourage our commitment to righteousness.

Much of the pressure we experience is peer pressure from coworkers, neighbors, and classmates. "Peer" refers to someone like this who is an "equal." But we also receive pressure from superiors—work supervisors, teachers, organizational leaders, and others—as well as general pressure from society as a whole. This chapter also has to do with these kinds of influences.

OUR MORAL ENVIRONMENT—PRESSURE UNLIMITED

To understand the intensity of pressure exerted by those around us, we need to understand something of the moral environment which these people constitute. Christians have always lived in nonChristian societies and have always been pressured to conform to the standards of their society. And believers in every era seem to feel their generation reflects more immorality than the last. Throughout history there have been those who said their generation was poised on the brink of moral chaos. Moreover, every generation is confronted with new moral issues. We may look at old books and magazines and be mildly amused at the things considered sinful many years ago. Yet as we review seriously the changing standards of the past decades we see clearly a sequence of degeneration.

In issues of morality and ethics, the general public and the church once held similar views. Such practices as sexual immorality, cheating, and lying were approved by neither the church nor the public. But in time the moral and ethical views of the public became increasingly liberal. Philosophies of moral freedom and rebellion rose to prominence. In government, the separation of church and state was emphasized more. In the arts, obscenity became more prevalent. Pornography grew into a multi-million-dollar business. The use of drugs and alcohol became a major problem—among youths as well as adults.

All the while Christians were deploring the trends—but ultimately they, too, conformed to them. For example, at one time most believers attended no movies. Later they occasionally attended less offensive ones. Today many have no qualms about attending R-rated movies to "see how the world is thinking." When skirt lengths climbed above the knee, most Christian women at first kept their hemlines low—that is, until the fashion industry dictated even shorter skirts, and Christians began following the trend although not quite to the extent dictated by contemporary fashion designers.

Christians have changed their thinking about more serious issues as well. Today we see a much broader range of opinions among believers on a variety of moral issues, from adultery to pornography and homosexuality.

Clearly, in a historical perspective, society has forced basic changes in almost every area of thought and conduct. Not all changes have been bad. Some of the old standards of behavior were legalistic, even ludicrous. But while some standards were wrong, many were biblical.

Today's environment is morally loose and ethically unstable. Although most public school administrators and teachers claim to be religiously neutral, they are essentially anti-religious because of the strong sway of humanistic philosophy in the colleges and universities where teachers are trained. Our laws, with their great focus on individual liberty, have been incapable of encouraging moral conduct. The "sexual revolution" is a reality that burrows deeper into teenagers' lives. The decline of religious influence and training has removed the moral foundation for society. And if the whole of the Christian community is swayed by the incredible pressure of society, imagine the effect also on many individual believers who usually conform to new standards a step ahead of the church as a whole.

Worldwide, the moral and ethical structure of society has accelerated enormously in the past few decades. Two basic causes have been increasing affluence and the impact of television.

As we become more affluent our focus moves from hard work and survival to personal pleasure and self-indulgence, a more fertile ground for weaker moral standards. But the real "mind-changer" is undoubtedly television. In recent years television has had at least as much influence on the education of young people as the schools. And while public schools have consciously backed off from teaching moral values, television programs reflect society's widespread acceptance of a new moral ideology—one that reflects increasingly lower standards. Many of the most popular programs have been those depicting family problems, divorces, adultery, and sexual deviation—often in the form of light, skillful comedy. They are amusing, but the first step in changing moral values comes when we laughingly accept such values in a fictional situation.

Many students spend more time watching television than they do in school. It has been estimated that a graduating senior has watched almost 15,000 hours of television (compared to 10,800 hours in school),[2] and that the average American spends between twenty-three and fifty hours a week watching television.[3] Television has more influence on some children than even their parents.

Our entire society is being impacted by the technological revolution in computers and information media. Video, compact discs, on-line services, and the worldwide web of the Internet are giving unprecedented access to vast information resources. Unfortunately, many children now have easy access to pornography and other harmful material. This is often material that parents are unaware of and do not know how to bar access. Add to that a growing children's rights movement that sometimes acts unjustly in the name of "protecting" children from their parents. Increasingly, parents find it more difficult to protect their children from the destructive inputs in these media. The result is an explosive influence in the entire life of the family and the moral future of a country.

With the enormous pressure of this input, much of it directly contrary to the teaching of Scripture, we soon begin to accept society's standards. We effectively become brainwashed. But society's standards cannot be the standards for Christians. We must realize that society applies this constant pressure on everyone to constantly lower our standards of morality and ethics.

These lower standards will be reflected especially by young adults and teenagers, who are always at the forefront of change. As moral foundations steadily erode, we must learn how to resist the conformity that causes us to no longer reflect scriptural principles for honest and ethical living.

The peer pressure we face is intricately connected with society's declining standards. To know how to live in society and survive morally unscathed we need to understand the sources of pressure, and to learn how to withstand and counteract the relentless push to conform.

WHAT IS CONFORMITY?

Martin wheeled into the parking lot by the office building. He was fifteen minutes early—but this was his first day on a new job. He walked into an almost vacant office. Most of the employees began arriving about ten minutes late and the boss came in twenty minutes late. *I guess there is no need to get here on time*, Martin thought. *I'll catch a couple of extra minutes of sleep tomorrow.* As the day went on he noticed that most of the men in the office wore sport coats. He was wearing a more formal blue suit. He made a mental note to dress more casually in the future. As he listened to the office talk he picked up some resentment for a particular section head. Before he realized it, Martin was resenting him too—though he had never met him.

Within a few weeks Martin had "adjusted" with little effort, so that he was almost a direct copy of the rest of the people in the office. We too conform without trying—almost without knowing it. We want to be accepted, and we are frightened by being too different.

Conformity can be voluntarily or inadvertently becoming like someone else. But Scripture tells us, "Do not be conformed to this world, but be transformed by the renewing of your mind" (Romans 12:2). Or, as J. B. Phillips paraphrases it, "Don't let the world around you squeeze you into its own mold, but let God remake you so that your whole attitude of mind is changed."

The biblical warning against conformity to the world concerns outward imitation or practices that are not consistent with the inner spiritual life of a Christian. Conformity to the world is to act, think, and speak like those in the world about us. To grasp the full impact of this thought, we must realize that the "world" spoken of in Scripture is anti-God and anti-Christian.

Peter instructed us, "As obedient children, do not be conformed to the former lusts which were yours in your ignorance" (1 Peter 1:14). Peter made this statement in a passage on holiness of life. Conformity to the moral standards of the world directly opposes holiness. Note that both these statements (Romans 12:2, 1 Peter 1:14) are direct commands—not just suggestions. We are commanded to be different from the world.

Some conformity is positive. The Bible speaks of conforming to Christ (Romans 8:29, Philippians 3:10), and this conformity reflects an inward transformation that has an outward effect. In contrast, the Greek word used in Romans 12:2 and 1 Peter 1:14 regarding conformity to the world means to masquerade outwardly contrary to the inner person.[4] Christ as Lord and Savior within our lives should affect every aspect of our outward lives. If Christ is present in us, conformity with the world is a cruel masquerade leading us to tension and inner turmoil.

THE KINDS OF CONFORMITY

We must battle against conformity in many areas of our lives. A few of the most obvious are:

Our mind. The first battlefield of conformity is the mind. We cannot speak or act unless the mind directs us. This is where outward conformity to the world begins.

We begin the mental process of conformity by desiring

to be like someone else, or to possess a position or material goods. Our minds play with these desires until certain cravings persist and become goals. Next we begin speaking or acting in such a way as to obtain these desired goals. Soon we are fully conformed in mind and action to obtaining them.

For example, if a person wishes to be accepted in a particular group of people, his mind begins dwelling on sample conversations and actions characteristic of the group. He then acts out the appropriate actions or speech when he is with the group. If the group swears and tells dirty jokes, he first rehearses such things in his mind and then acts them out, practicing conformity to be accepted.

We must understand the difference between thinking the "things" the world thinks, and thinking the "way" the world thinks. The first is incidental and specific. The second is a process and a pattern. Everyone at times experiences lustful thoughts or unwise actions. Danger comes when these are a continual pattern, and lead us mentally to the world's conclusions instead of a recognition and confession of sin. Wanting living room furniture or a new car is one thing. To have a materialistic coveting for them is another. In the same way, to commit a prideful act is quite different from governing one's life with selfish motives.

Specific incidents of conformity in our lives are relatively easy to detect. The development of the world's pattern of thinking, however, is deceptive, subtle, and dangerous. Increasingly, the world's thinking rejects the existence of absolute moral standards. "'[There is] a growing degree of cynicism and sophistication in our society,' says Jody Powell, former press secretary to Jimmy Carter, 'a sense that all things are relative and that nothing is absolutely right.'"5

Without objective standards, what seems right or feels good becomes the criteria by which decisions are made and justified. Though many believers recognize the dangers of relative thinking, this self-gratifying aspect of relativism creeps into our thoughts, appealing to our sinful nature. We must submit our minds to God's Word, allowing our thinking to be conformed to His. This is the only defense against the subtle attractions of a relativistic mindset, which recognizes no rights or wrongs, a mindset that both tempts me to sin and excuses me afterward.

For this reason we must test the philosophies and opinions of nonChristian educators, politicians, entertainers, theologians, and other influential persons against the measure of Scripture. Both television and the educational system — elementary, high school, and college — are critical mind-shaping tools that can either build up or warp the minds of young people.

Conformity of mind to a totally secular society will eat away the very foundation of biblical teaching and action. "Let this *mind* be in you, which was also in Christ Jesus," Paul told the Philippians. "Whatever is true, whatever is honorable, whatever is right, whatever is pure, whatever is lovely, whatever is of good repute, if there is any excellence and if anything worthy of praise, let your *mind* dwell on these things" (Philippians 2:5, KJV; 4:8, emphasis added).

Our speech. Listen to yourself talk when you are around nonbelievers. Can you detect differences in what you say and how you say it, compared to what you say around believers? To your amazement a swear word may even slip in, along with other crude or unkind speech, sarcasm, and criticism.

Depending on who we're with, the driving desire to "fit in" leads us to speak in ways that are tough, intellectual, frivolous, knowledgeable, or crude. This same disparity between who we really are and how we speak occurs even in Christian circles, where our speech may be spiritual, kind, or scriptural, although that may not describe our inward condition at all.

We should not confuse conformity with consideration

and politeness. We are not to offend others by our speech just so we can "be our real selves." We are to speak courteously and in a pleasing way—but not simply to be part of the crowd.

Deep friendships cannot develop when our conversations are marked by cutting remarks, jokes at someone else's expense, wisecracks, and quick comebacks. We are commanded, "Let no unwholesome word proceed from your mouth, but only such a word as is good for edification according to the need of the moment" (Ephesians 4:29).

Our actions. The most observable aspects of our lives are speech and actions—and of the two, actions speak louder.

Again, mentally step out of your body and observe how you conduct yourself in the context of various groups—people at church, the people at work, and others. What differences do you see? Do you blend in like a chameleon in either place? Are you able to keep your personality intact in both groups?

Watch how a teenager acts in the home, in a classroom, and with friends. He appears to be three different people. Adults also have such differences in behavior, but they camouflage them a little better.

Are your actions consistent with what you believe? Or does the group you are with determine how you respond and behave?

Our lifestyle. The drive to "keep up with the Joneses" has become the American way of life. What others have, we want. If we can possibly afford it, we buy it. A pay raise means a new car, a larger house, a boat, or a vacation. We push for "upward mobility"—climbing the socio-economic ladder. Even Christians adopt these lifestyle characteristics. We often equate God's blessing with material gain—and make that our goal.

Lifestyle involves some distinct philosophies of life. How

well should we live? Do we really seek God's direction in lifestyle, or simply conform to the limit of our financial ability? Is there anything in our lifestyle that distinguishes us as believers in Christ? We may not need to make a vow of poverty, but we must ask what distinguishes us from the world.

When you make the next "upward" move, carefully consider the implications and reasons behind it. Don't let simple conformity to the rest of society determine your lifestyle.

SOURCES OF THE PRESSURE TO CONFORM

The pressure to conform comes from many sources and directions. Three of these especially have major influence.

Individual peers. We all have friends or acquaintances who exert great influence over our thinking. We are swayed by their ideas and suggestions, sometimes to the exclusion of our own. "But Rich said . . ." settles any dilemma in the mind if Rich is the main influence in our lives. We need to consciously realize who these individuals are, and be certain their influence is positive. We must carefully choose our close friends—and also observe and guard the influence we have on others.

Groups. Several distinct groups usually have a major influence on us—our church, coworkers, clubs, friends, neighbors, sports partners, and others. Each group applies pressure to make us act and believe in a certain way. Group dynamics can make an individual do things he would never think of doing on his own. "There is safety in numbers," we may say, or, "If everyone is doing it, it must be okay."

We must resist the influences of groups with which we cannot morally and ethically agree, and avoid rushing into decisions and actions because of group pressure.

Business. The pressure of management and the drive to produce can push people to acts, words, and thoughts they never dreamed possible. Ethics are broken, principles are bent, harsh words are spoken, and the pressure is passed on to subordinates. We may become conformed to the tactics of people we least want to imitate.

HOW TO WITHSTAND PRESSURE FROM OTHERS
Despite the magnitude of the pressure we face from others, there are practical things we can do in dealing with it.

Be honest. We are all affected by this pressure more than we like to admit, and we need to honestly admit our tendency to succumb to it. Admit this first to yourself and then to God—then perhaps to others who are close to you. Recognizing that you talk or act differently in particular situations, for example, or that you are subject to being taken in by worldly advertising, is a sign of maturity.

Check your own spiritual moorings. Check the state of your own spiritual life. Is there sin you have been reluctant to deal with? Are you reading and studying the Bible regularly? Are you praying about your circumstances? Are you being obedient to God in what He wants you to do? Are you fulfilling scriptural responsibilities in your home?

If there is a major need in one of these areas, work on it first. Later you can handle the problem of pressure from others.

Develop personal convictions. Have you developed many personal convictions for yourself in such areas as lifestyle, speech, and thought life? Convictions are a foundation for resisting pressure to conform to wrong actions or speech.

Recognize the sources of pressure. When you sense pressure to conform, search out the source. Is it a friend, a group, a boss? When you know the source you can determine if the pressure is harmful and what you should do about it.

Don't give in. Resist drastic changes in your actions and speech. Determine in advance that you will take a personal stand on key issues—those in which you are easily tempted to sin.

Speak up. Don't be afraid to let your personal convictions be known. In areas of honesty and morality, suggest a right direction for the good of others. Don't waste time trying to change nonbelievers in such areas as smoking, drinking, and bad language, but confront more important issues of honesty and ethical decisions.

Be consistent. If you make your convictions known, you are obligated to live a life consistent with them. Avoid vacillation on issues. Follow your convictions without being obstinate and unreasonable. People will watch carefully to see how you resist conformity.

Be an influence. Learn to influence others rather than being influenced by them. Whether you are a natural leader or not, your decisions can have a great impact on the lives of others. Some may be waiting for you to oppose the crowd and to give them enough courage to also resist conformity.

Run. When all else fails in your battle against conformity, run. One of the best military maneuvers in the face of overwhelming odds is retreat. When you know you cannot resist or influence others, you need to get out of the situation. "Do not enter the path of the wicked, and do not proceed in the way of evil men. Avoid it, do not pass by it; turn away from it and pass on" (Proverbs 4:14-15).

Notes

1. Emile Henry Gauvreau, as quoted in *The International Encyclopedia of Quotations* (Chicago: J. G. Ferguson Publishing, 1975), p. 158.
2. Mel White, "Only You Can Fight the Boob Tube," *Eternity*, December 1973, p. 15.
3. This statistical range was compiled from three sources: *Statistical Abtract of the United States*, table 884 (Lanham, Md.: Bernan Press, 1994), p. 568; *TV and Video Almanac, 1995* (New York: Quigley Publishing, 1995), p. 20A; William J. Bennet, *The Index of Leading Cultural Indicators*, vol. 1 (The Heritage Foundation and Empower America, 1993).
4. Kenneth S. Wuest, *Word Studies in the Greek New Testament* (Grand Rapids, Mich.: Eerdmans, 1955), vol. 1, pp. 145, 206-207.
5. "A Nation of Liars," *US News and World Report*, 27 February 1987.

Chapter Six

HONESTY AND ETHICS IN BUSINESS AND WORK

───────────── ∽ ─────────────

Douglas Aircraft Company (now McDonnell Douglas Astronautics) was competing with Boeing Aircraft Company to sell Eastern Airlines its first big jets. Eddie Rickenbacker, the head of Eastern Airlines, reportedly told Donald Douglas that the specifications and claims made by Douglas's company for the DC-8 were close to Boeing's on everything except noise suppression. Rickenbacker then gave Douglas one last chance to out-promise Boeing on this feature.

"After consulting his engineers, Douglas reported back that he did not feel he could make that promise. Rickenbacker replied, 'I know you can't. I wanted to see if you were still honest. You just got yourself an order for $135 million. Now go home and silence those jets!'"[1]

Honesty does pay!

Perhaps the stakes in our life and work are not as high as $135 million, but we often expect a profit from being dishonest. Why else would we take the risk? The payoff of dishonesty must be significant enough to cause us to violate known standards and laws. It may be career, reputation, avoiding conflict, avoiding embarrassment, or getting money. What would it take to make you dishonest?

A story is told of a man who was asked if he would lie about a particular matter. He gave a resounding "No!"

"What if I gave you ten dollars?"

"Absolutely not!"

"How about for twenty-five dollars?"

"Definitely not!"

"One hundred dollars?"

"No!" he still persisted.

"One thousand?"

"Well . . . maybe I could. . . ."

Everyone has his price. Find a person's weak point and he will lie, cheat, or steal — if the price or pressure proves sizable enough.

But usually the temptation is more subtle than simple. The temptation to be dishonest or unethical sneaks quietly into our lives. Temptation surprises us because it comes from a totally unexpected source such as a friend or trusted coworker. Temptation comes dressed in cloaks of urgency and accepted practice. Rarely does it attack frontally, but often it develops through a series of small compromises. Temptation can be disguised by a sense of obligation or loyalty.

In business and work, other people's standards tend to become ours. We hear so many arguments for "accepted practice" that we begin to believe them — even when we know the accepted practice is questionable. Why make a fuss over "little" things that really don't matter? After all, the company plans for some of those little losses.

- Can we be totally honest in our jobs?
- Can a businessman be really honest and still succeed?
- Do we cheat the company by wasting time on the job?

- How much should a believer in Christ become involved in the power struggles and politics of a company?
- Are company regulations really law?
- Must we obey our employer when it is wrong to do what he asks?
- How can we confront dishonesty in the company and other workers—or should we?

Fortunately, we do have guidelines for knowing what to do—from God's perspective—in specific situations.

FIVE COMMANDS FOR BUSINESS ETHICS

Ethics is a word that means whatever you want it to mean. Most politicians and businessmen would say they are ethical. But a precise definition for the word would not guide us into ethical behavior anyway. It would simply define right and wrong based on a set of "ethical standards." Most professions maintain a written or unwritten code of ethics. The code may have no real relationship to right or wrong, but simply outline accepted conduct and practice.

We cannot depend on the world's standard of ethics for our personal lives. We need a more sure base of belief for our conduct. This base can be found in the Bible, the conscience, and the particular leading of God in an individual's life.

But simply knowing what the Bible says and what God wants is not sufficient. We must do it. Knowledge is no substitute for action. "To one who knows the right thing to do, and does not do it, to him it is sin" (James 4:17).

Ethics to the government is *law*. Ethics to the philosopher is a *concept*. Ethics to religion is *morality*. But ethics to God is *obedience*.

We must remember that every ethical decision is

ultimately a decision of the will. We must know what is right and *do* what we know is right. Knowing what the Bible says is a first step to obedience.

A JUST WEIGHT

God commanded Israel, "You shall not have in your bag differing weights, a large and a small. You shall not have in your house differing measures, a large and a small. You shall have a full and just weight; you shall have a full and just measure, that your days may be prolonged in the land which the Lord your God gives you" (Deuteronomy 25:13-15).

This concept of a just weight is found many times in the Old Testament. On a balance scale the proper weight of a product is determined by placing balancing weights on the other side of the scale. Cheating can occur when similar-sized pieces that vary in weight are used. In this manner a few ounces less could be given for the full price. A similar practice with modern scales would be to add a little pressure to the scale with your thumb to make the scale register higher.

The principal issue is to give the full amount in exchange for a fair payment. Also it is to give full quality for what is paid for and according to what is advertised. Honesty extends to quality as well as amount. Honesty requires a believer to sell not "what the market will bear" or even what the market "demands" if the product or service is questionable. A Christian businessman must accept responsibility for the quality of his product as well as establish a fair price. To represent a product of inferior quality as equal to one of known higher quality is an "unjust weight."

In the American culture deceptive advertising has become an accepted practice. But, more disturbing, Christians have been influenced by this practice and follow it out of competitive self-defense. Believers must be willing to risk the loss of business to maintain a clear conscience. Although a reputation based on honesty and true quality will always benefit a business, such a reputation takes time to build.

Now look at the matter of a just weight from another viewpoint: What is an employee's responsibility to an employer? A Christian employee is bound by Scripture to give a full day's work for a full day's pay. He is also obligated to do his work in the way he is directed—to produce an acceptable product.

Can a believer, in clear conscience, participate in a "work slowdown" or purposely degrade the quality of his work? The scriptural answer is "no." We are responsible to do our best and to be obedient to our employers. Paul said, "Whatever you do, do your work heartily, as for the Lord rather than for men" (Colossians 3:23). He said slaves were to do their work "not by way of eye service, as men-pleasers, but as slaves of Christ, doing the will of God from the heart. With good will render service, as to the Lord, and not to men" (Ephesians 6:6-7).

Circumstances may occur where the employer is truly unjust or dishonest. In such cases there are legal ways to voice grievances and change the situation.

TOTAL HONESTY

Can we be totally honest without becoming overly burdened about the absolute truthfulness of every minor issue? What do we mean by total honesty?

James said, "We all stumble in many ways. If anyone does not stumble in what he says, he is a perfect man, able to bridle the whole body as well" (James 3:2). This statement has two thoughts of particular interest. First, we cannot keep from sinning with the tongue. Even when we intend to speak the truth, we often slip and state a half-truth or even a lie. Then our pride raises a stumbling block and the lie remains uncorrected. The second thought is that if we guard and control our tongues, we can control the entire body! Think of the magnitude of this. What a motivation to control the tongue! This statement from James assures us that if our tongues are controlled, our thoughts, motives, and actions are also under control.

To the best of our knowledge, we must speak the truth to everyone. Paul said, "Respect what is right in the sight of all men" (Romans 12:17). Or, as *The Living Bible* paraphrases it, "Do things in such a way that everyone can see you are honest clear through."

Paul wrote to the Ephesians to lay aside falsehood and to "speak truth, each one of you, with his neighbor, for we are members of one another" (Ephesians 4:25). And who is our neighbor? Jesus answered that question with the parable of the good Samaritan, showing that we are obligated to be neighborly to all. We must speak truthfully—to everyone.

Although we will frequently fail, our intent must be total honesty with our employer, our coworkers, our employees, and our customers. An employee must be totally honest with his employer in the use of time, in reporting what has been accomplished (or hasn't been accomplished), in stating his ability to do a specific task, in projections of what will be accomplished, in reporting business expenses, and in many other things.

Likewise, an employer has an obligation for total honesty with his employees or subordinates. The Levitical Law states, "You shall not steal, nor deal falsely, nor lie to one another . . . You shall not oppress your neighbor, nor rob him. The wages of a hired man are not to remain with you all night until morning" (Leviticus 19:11,13). To withhold wages, to deceive an employee about pay or job potential, or in any other way to defraud an employee is being untruthful. An employer has the authority and freedom to do what is right. One of the key marks of a *Christian* businessman is total honesty.

Honesty with customers is good business. But what

about *total* honesty, especially with customers who cannot know the real value or quality of a product? Should you volunteer information? Scripturally you must do so, even though you may lose a sale.

Recently, I dealt with a salesman who would *not* sell me a particular product because he was convinced it would not meet my needs. I was ignorant about the product's quality and features. I sensed that the salesman was concerned for me and not just with making a sale. Christians are under an obligation to deal this honestly with every customer. This, of course, forces us to evaluate our product in both quality and price. It is not wrong to produce and handle items of lower quality, but advertising and selling them as higher quality merchandise is deceptive.

THE LAW OF SERVING

Believers in Christ are to be servants of both God and people. But most of us approach business and work — and life in general — with the attitude "What can I *get*?" rather than "What can I *give*?"

We find it encouraging to think of ourselves as God's servants. Who would not want to be a servant of the King? But when it comes to serving other people, we begin to question the consequences. We feel noble when serving God; we feel humble when serving people. Serving God receives a favorable response; serving people, especially those who cannot repay, has no visible benefit or glory from anyone — except from God! Christ gave us the example: "The Son of Man did not come to be served, but to serve, and to give His life a ransom for many" (Matthew 20:28). To be a servant of God we must be a servant of people.

In business and work the concept of serving people must undergird all that we do. When we serve we think first of the one we are trying to serve. An employee who serves honestly in his work honors God and deepens his value to his employer. On the other hand, the self-serving employee will seldom be valued in any company.

Service is a key word in any business. But serving without the goal of a sale is quite another matter. We need always to aim to meet the needs of another — to operate in his best interests. If we put our customers' interests first, and genuinely attempt to serve them, we will experience God's blessing in our lives and work.

Personal Responsibility

"It's really not my fault," we may say, "because company policies and practices force me to operate in this manner." How often we try to shift responsibility for questionable or even dishonest actions to the company or someone else. Every company has ethical "soft spots" which have developed as standard practices over the years. But that does not excuse the Christian employee in any way. We are all responsible for our own actions and decisions. A watchword of a believer's business ethics must be *personal responsibility*. James said, "Each one is tempted when he is carried away and enticed by his own lust" (James 1:14).

We are totally responsible for our own actions, not only before God, but in every court of law. When we compromise our ethics, we can blame only ourselves. Let us not be lulled into conformity with the world's practices. Every Christian is warned, "Don't let the world around you squeeze you into its own mold" (Romans 12:2, PH).

In accepting responsibility for our actions we may encounter conflict with our supervisors and others in the company. But when we compromise our ethics and conscience, we sacrifice part of our very life and being.

Former presidential aide Jeb Stuart Magruder, commenting on the Watergate scandal, said, "We had conned ourselves into thinking we weren't doing anything really wrong, and by the time we were doing things that were illegal, we had lost control. We had gone from poor ethical behavior into illegal activities without even realizing it."[2]

In opposing practices that are unethical or dishonest we may risk losing a job. But if the company is determined to follow questionable practices, we probably do not want to continue working for them. Our conscience will quickly be dulled if we must constantly try to justify our actions.

REASONABLE PROFIT

Of these five guidelines, reasonable profit may be the most difficult to describe, define, and defend. Consumers want to give the producer as little profit as possible. Businessmen know that profit is vital for their business to survive. Some items need a larger profit to make up for less profitable or slow-moving items. So the seller's definition of "reasonable" may differ from his customer's.

William Krutza tells about a Christian real estate investor who boasted, "I don't go into any deals unless I can make 500 to 2,000 percent profit! Simply find someone who does not know the value of his property or who is anxious to get rid of it for financial reasons. Never tell a seller the potential for the property . . . or of the deal you are planning."[3]

Krutza concluded that most Christian businessmen operate on the same basis as nonChristians—profit, products, people, and principle, in that order.

We cannot define monetarily a reasonable profit that would apply to all situations. Each businessman must seriously grapple with that issue in his own circumstances. Certainly the oft quoted and seldom applied "golden rule" gives significant guidance: "Just as you want men to treat you, treat them in the same way" (Luke 6:31). The seller needs to imagine himself on the purchasing end and ask if the price is just and fair.

Reasonable profit and *reasonable wages* are inseparable. Are we willing to be satisfied with our wages, or do we always

want more no matter how much we get now? What a reasonable profit is to a businessman, so must a reasonable
wage be to the employee.

The words of John the Baptist to some soldiers apply also
to employees today: "Do not take money from anyone by force,
or accuse anyone falsely, and be content with your wages"
(Luke 3:14). A believer's chief end is not self-profit. He acts
differently. He can be content. Should he never ask for a raise?
He may ask, but he must be satisfied with wages that are a just
and fair return on the time and effort he has invested.

The employer also has a scriptural mandate to pay a just
wage, for "the laborer is worthy of his wages" (1 Timothy
5:18; see also Leviticus 19:13). In fact, is this not the balance of profit and wages — the sharing of profit with those
who make it possible?

A just profit and a just wage are two key principles of a
Christian in business.

TYPICAL PROBLEMS

Many problems related to honesty in business and work
repeat themselves so frequently and persistently that they
deserve special attention. A few are listed here to jog your
thinking and conscience as you examine your own situation
and earnestly seek God's direction.

OBEYING THE LAW

Every nation passes laws governing the lives of its citizens.
Many of these laws actually originated with scriptural teaching, particularly the Ten Commandments. Others have developed over the centuries as necessity demanded.

We are bound to keep these laws: "Let every person be
in subjection to the governing authorities. . . . For rulers are
not a cause of fear for good behavior, but for evil. Do you
want to have no fear of authority? Do what is good, and you

will have praise from the same" (Romans 13:1,3). Even Jesus obeyed the Roman law—from paying taxes to submitting to crucifixion.

These laws are only a limited guideline for a believer. What is legal may not be ethical or right. We operate under a higher and more just law—the law of God. But those in business who follow Christ are obligated to obey secular law to the best of their knowledge and ability, not allowing expediency or peer pressure to push them into illegal activities and dealings.

We must establish our principles in small things to prepare us for large decisions. Recently I made an offer to purchase a travel trailer. The seller told me he could write a smaller amount on the bill of sale than the actual sale price, so I would pay less tax. I immediately told him I would not consider that. If I hadn't decided that, disobeying the law in larger matters would be much easier in the future.

Contempt and disregard for the law have become chronic. Many in our society obey laws only when it fits their agenda conveniently. Obedience to the law—and to a set of absolute values greater than ourselves—has taken a back seat to personal gain and situational ethics. "There is a sullen cynicism in the air, so pervasive that Harvard University sociologist David Riesman has warned that Americans are approaching the point where the prevailing ethic is: 'You're a fool to follow the rules.'"[4]

Some believers operate on the very edge of the law—legal, but barely. The edge soon becomes fuzzy and slips into illegality. Our conscience and our testimony must be guarded.

MISREPRESENTATION

Misrepresentation is making people believe that a product or a service is better than it really is.

A Christian physician in a western city was a member of

a unified health coalition in which all the doctors in the city treated patients at specified rates. Each doctor was then rated and evaluated by his peers. During this evaluation, the physicians found that this doctor had administered unnecessary treatment, had overcharged his patients, and had even charged for services he had not performed. Because of his unethical practices, he was asked to leave the health coalition. He endangered the reputation of his profession and certainly that of the local body of believers. He had misrepresented his services and integrity.

In reality, misrepresentation is a nice word for lying. For example, the drive to make a sale can easily obscure sensitivity to truth. Withholding crucial information about a used car, representing an inferior product as equal to another, suggesting qualities about yourself or your abilities that are not true, faking activity on a job without accomplishing anything, and promising delivery and performance that you know are impossible—all are ways of misrepresenting the facts.

We cannot allow ourselves to fall into the trap of thinking we must shade the truth to survive. We cannot—and still have a clear conscience and God's blessing. We may not get caught and may even increase our earnings, but is it worth it?

COMPROMISE AND CONDONING DISHONESTY

At the United States Air Force Academy a faculty officer caught a student illegally possessing liquor. After reprimanding him sharply and removing the liquor, he told the cadet that he would not report him, but made him promise never to break the regulation again. The officer was trying to show compassion, since in the academy system the student would have encountered severe discipline if his violation had been reported. Most of us would consider the officer gracious and sympathetic.

A few months later the same cadet was caught with liquor

in his room. When confronted with the offense, he said that this officer had caught him previously but didn't report it. Within days the officer was transferred from the academy, his assignment terminated and his career blemished.

Moses warned the Hebrews, "Be sure your sin will find you out" (Numbers 32:23). If we begin compromising in moral and ethical issues, we form dangerous habits. Compromise with sin in our own lives results when we condone the wrong actions and practices of others. We condone sin when we know and approve the misdeeds of others. We compromise when we do it ourselves.

People will frequently reveal their small unethical actions to check our reactions to them. They watch carefully to see if we will condone what they do. If we object, we will usually not be confronted by them again. But if we give silent agreement, we will find ourselves drawn into situations that compromise our convictions and reputation.

How frequently does compromise confront the normal person? According to one report by the American Management Associations, about 70 percent of nearly 3,000 businessmen surveyed said that they were expected at least occasionally to compromise their principles to conform to their company's or boss's standards. "Moreover, they ranked 'reputation for firm moral and/or ethical convictions' at the bottom of a list of factors considered in awarding promotions, behind 'family and ethnic background' and far to the rear of 'personal contacts ("who you know").'"[5]

Your background may not have provided you with sound convictions to help you guard against compromise. You may not know what is right and wrong because of the overpowering influence in your life of peers who operate unethically. If so, you must seek advice from reliable Christian friends and study the Bible to develop your own personal convictions.

Ignorance is no excuse for doing wrong. Each person bears responsibility before God for his actions. Believers are responsible to *know* how God wants them to live and believe. And beyond knowledge, followers of Christ must *do* what they know.

Condoning and compromising are time bombs in the Christian life. At an unexpected moment they explode and begin a destructive process.

CONFRONTING DISHONESTY

While I was on the faculty at the United States Air Force Academy, I answered a newspaper ad to buy a used item, and visited the home of the seller. As I walked in, I noticed some teenagers in the dining room laughing, playing games, and eating. When the seller found out I was on the academy faculty, he told me proudly that his son was a freshman there. Then, rather jokingly, he said that his son was in the dining room and was home from the academy against regulations. I have no idea why he told me this, but it put me in an awkward position. If I did not report the violation, no one would know the difference. But I was concerned that this young man who was training to be an officer in the United States Air Force was already cheating the system.

After prayer and some struggle, I called the cadet's commanding officer and informed him of this circumstance. This young man had an excellent reputation at the academy. I found out that he was one of the top freshman students, and was scheduled to command the freshmen contingent during a holiday period when all the upperclassmen commanders were gone. Of course, he was denied that command after his violation was reported.

No one likes to confront dishonesty. We would rather ignore it and hope someone else will discover it. Confrontation usually brings conflict and difficult relationships. But Christians must influence the workplace morality and ethics of their coworkers. This confrontation is essential since we must stand up for what is honest and right.

Of course, not everyone agrees with the necessity of confronting wrong. One retired chief executive of a large nationwide firm said, "My advice would be to mind your own business if it's a minor matter. In the first place, I don't believe in imposing my morality on somebody else. Besides, little things like padding expense accounts are built into corporations. They're safety valves, little ways people can get back because they feel exploited in some way."[6] But believers cannot go along with this viewpoint.

John A. Howard puts his finger on the real issue: "There is no such thing as moral neutrality. Those who do not stand up forthrightly in behalf of their convictions, by their inaction are supporting the opposite view. On any scale whenever a person perceives right and wrong, silence turns out to be a vote for wrong."[7]

But how can we confront in an effective and helpful way, rather than being harsh and antagonizing? Here are some guidelines:

1. Be certain your facts are correct.
2. Discern between personal preferences and unethical or illegal behavior. Smoking in a non-smoking area is discourteous, but rarely would there be legal consequences. On the other hand, lying to clients or cheating on expense accounts are serious issues.
3. Make written notes beforehand to help reduce emotional interaction at the time of confrontation.
4. Discern between isolated instances and habit patterns.
5. Pray about what action to take. Seek God's direction.
6. Unless it is an illegal matter (such as embezzlement or bribery), go to the person involved and

share informally your personal observations and concern. Do not accuse, but simply state your observations and ask for information to be sure you are correct. (Admittedly, this is risky in terms of inciting a bad reaction, but in most cases it is the right thing to do.) Use tact and diplomacy.

7. If necessary, go to the person's supervisor. Use the line of authority designated by your company.

8. Make sure you have nothing to gain by exposing the person's problems.

9. If you are wrong, apologize and clear it up with anyone you may have told.

10. If the person is your employer or supervisor, the situation is especially sensitive. Paul M. Hammaker, a former president of Montgomery Ward, advises this approach: "You say, 'Boss, I'd like some advice. There's something you're doing that bothers me, but maybe my standards are cockeyed. Explain it so I'll understand.' Most bosses won't fire you on the spot. If he won't discuss it, then I think it's time to look for a job with another company."[8]

OBEYING YOUR EMPLOYER

Your employer may require you to do something unethical or illegal, especially if you have developed the habit and reputation of compromise and condoning.

I have a friend who works in the headquarters of a large business handling hardware and other merchandise. He makes purchases for the company. His job requires him to give reports to the company's major distributors. These reports determine discounts based on the volume turnover of their product. On one occasion his supervisor instructed him to include a previous report with his current monthly report because it would give a particular advantage in terms of buying price. My friend would thus have to sign a false report. The supervisor assured him that he had talked to the company representative and they had agreed this was proper. However, my friend was troubled by the dishonesty involved, and the next day he again asked his supervisor about it. The supervisor again said this was exactly the way it ought to be done. But my friend's conscience bothered him. After obtaining more information on the account, and much prayer, claiming Proverbs 21:1, he decided to maintain his own integrity. He refused to include the previous month's figures on his report, and his supervisor grudgingly concurred. He risked his job for what he believed was right, and he was later promoted.

Such commitment to God results in the moral courage necessary to maintain our integrity in difficult situations, as in the previous example. Commitment to integrity means we have chosen to operate from "standards of moral and intellectual honesty . . . from which we cannot swerve without cheapening our better selves."[9]

This example illustrates the limit of authority. No authority can force you to violate your convictions and cause you to sin. If those in authority force an unethical situation, resignation is the answer. When confronted with a decision, refuse immediately. Don't think it over or give long explanations. It is risky, but have faith in God, trusting Him to protect you.

REGULATIONS

Company regulations are not statements of law, but simply company policy. They are not always right, but are simply part of the contract of employment. Many regulations are absurd and almost impossible to obey fully—especially in government or military operations.

As a young Air Force officer, I was at one time temporarily assigned to the civil engineering section at a particular base. I inspected the work done by contractors and certified that they had completed a certain portion of the work so they could receive partial payments.

While inspecting one building, I found that the electrical work was not in progress and had only been partially completed. Therefore, I reported that no work had been accomplished. Apparently the contractor expected me to report that some work had been completed so he could get payment. He was very upset and rushed into my commander's office to complain. Fortunately, the commander supported me and refused to change the report.

In another circumstance, several Christian officers served as missile launch officers at an Air Force base. In the process of taking training and passing a certain examination, they were required to record that they had spent a certain number of hours in a trainer. When the exercise could be completed in a shorter length of time, it was common practice to record the full number of hours. They felt this was dishonest since it misrepresented the number of hours.

They protested the practice even though their complaints implied that others were dishonest. After talking with a number of superior officers responsible for setting up the tests, they were assured that the intent of the regulation was to have the officers complete the work and become proficient—not necessarily to put in a particular number of hours.

Certain regulations are impossible to keep fully. For instance, there are multiple volumes of regulations covering every aspect of government contracts. Contracting officers must attest that all contracts meet these regulations. To do so perfectly would take months or years of checking. Therefore, there must be a working agreement with the originators that the regulations are being followed to the best of their ability, and a spot check must be sufficient. Then, a document saying that the specifications are met can be signed by those who know that the *intent* of the regulations has been met.

THE LITTLE THINGS

Most of us do not grapple with flagrant instances of cheating, lying, or stealing. But we do struggle with little things—truthfulness on expense accounts, personal use of office supplies and long distance phone calls, and honestly reporting work accomplishments. But we must be scrupulous in our attention to honesty and ethics in these small matters. Office things belong at the office. Admittedly, personal and business matters are almost inextricably intertwined in certain jobs. Some companies allow personal benefits from company equipment. But these benefits should be clearly outlined.

While writing a previous book, I asked my secretary to do the typing, and I used a copy machine and supplies from our organization's office. The secretary kept a record of her time and expenses and I subsequently reimbursed these costs. I might have considered the work to be job-related since it was closely related to my speaking and ministry. But I would not have had a clear conscience since I did reap financial benefits for the publication. On another book, written for the United States Air Force Academy, I received no payment so I had no reason to keep similar records.

Develop ethical habits with little things and you will build a solid base for the big decisions.

USE OF TIME

Management Review reported that 80 percent of all employees are guilty of stealing time and that the average "theft" is three hours and forty-five minutes a week.[10] Believers are honor-bound to give a day's work for a day's pay, and to do the work properly. We must offer the employer both time and accomplishment.

We all know when we are wasting our employer's time. When I taught at the Air Force Academy, I had considerable freedom in daily scheduling. As a result I often counseled cadets on spiritual matters. At times I became convicted that I might not be giving the Air Force its fair amount of time. Therefore, I began to keep a log of the time I spent in actual Air Force work to keep a realistic and balanced assessment of my time use.

We need to be careful not to cheat our employer by the deliberate waste of time. This, of course, requires common sense judgment in many types of jobs. A machine operator on a factory assembly line may be extremely proficient, for example, and therefore be ahead of the line schedule. He is not deliberately wasting time as he waits. And many management jobs frequently allow considerable flexibility in time use.

POLITICS, POWER, AND PERSONAL FRIENDSHIPS

The saying "It's not what you know but who you know that counts" carries good substantiation in the world, but its application can lead to highly unethical practices. Most companies have a political structure and some employees exploit it to full advantage. In some situations the "politics" involves trading favors and monetary kickbacks. But it is dishonest to develop relationships for the express purpose of using a person in a political way. We must not succumb to such maneuvers for the sake of a promotion or raise.

Similarly, one who is in a position of power and authority can easily misuse that power. The more power and authority a person has, the more he must guard his motives and ethics in every situation. We've witnessed gross abuse of power in the past twenty-five years: Watergate, the Iran-Contra affair, the Whitewater controversy, and multiple ethical breaches by others in power. Given power over people and money, we are all tempted to use it unethically.

Jesus said, "You know that the rulers of the Gentiles lord it over them, and their great men exercise authority over them. It is not so among you, but whoever wishes to become great among you shall be your servant" (Matthew 20:25-26).

HOW TO MAKE ETHICAL DECISIONS IN BUSINESS AND WORK

In this chapter you may have been stimulated to think of issues and problems in your own life that may be unethical, but the *exact* answer for your situation was not given. We seldom find a universal answer, except for the wrongness of such things as flagrant illegality, lying, or cheating. Yet we must continually make decisions with ethical implications. How we make these decisions now will determine how we conduct ourselves for years to come. The guidelines listed below can help us make these decisions correctly.

Get the facts. Be certain you have all the relevant facts about the issue at stake. Feelings can never replace facts. What did your boss ask you to do? What is the law? What are the company's regulations? What are you doing that is questionable? What finances are involved? Write out the pertinent facts, especially if you are struggling with a major decision.

Search the Bible. Check the Bible for specific instructions in these decisions.

Examine your personal life. Consider your spiritual life. Are you reading the Bible and praying daily? If you are not, there is danger in totally trusting your own judgment, and you must rely more heavily on the counsel of others. Are you a new Christian or a Christian who has not grown spiritually? If so, you may have habit patterns that have dulled your conscience, and you will need to act more conservatively. I once talked with a new Christian who was very successful in large real estate and financial dealings. He told me that the methods and style of his dealings were such that he simply could not continue to operate now that he was a Christian. He knew he had to rebuild his foundations for decision making.

Know accepted standards. Be aware of the accepted standards of your profession. Areas that are neither unethical nor illegal may be restricted by these standards. However, do not allow the standards to govern you when they are ethically questionable.

Listen to your conscience. When the Bible does not speak directly to an issue, carefully write out what your conscience is impressing upon you. Align your conscience with Scripture.

Pray. Now take all these facts to God in prayer. His Word promises, "If any of you lacks wisdom, let him ask of God, who gives to all men generously and without reproach, and it will be given to him" (James 1:5). You need wisdom to make the right decision. God will lead you as you pray about specific issues.

Seek counsel. Many times we do not know enough Scripture, our experience is quite limited, or we are so subjectively involved that we lose perspective. Then counsel from a godly, trusted friend can be of great help. It is even more helpful when this friend has been in similar circumstances. Frequently, you may want to seek counsel from more than one person. Remember that no one is infallible and only you can make the decision. No one else can bear your responsibility.

Take a few minutes now to write down some of your basic convictions in the area of honesty and ethics. What situations have you personally encountered in which you have made foundational decisions?

Can a Christian be totally honest? Yes. But wavering and compromising will destroy our attempts to be honest. We must establish basic guidelines for honesty in our life and job, and follow them.

Notes

1. *Bits and Pieces*, October 1976, pp. 6-7.
2. Jeb Stuart Magruder, "Will Success Spoil the Corporate Christian?" *Eternity*, September 1976, p. 21.
3. William J. Krutza, "The Nearsighted Ethics of Christian Business-men," *Eternity*, September 1976, p. 16.
4. "The Sense of Morality," *Royal Bank Letter*, vol. 65, no. 1, January/February 1984 (Royal Bank of Canada).
5. Avery Comarow, "When Conscience and Career Collide," *Money*, September 1976, pp. 49-50.
6. Comarow, "When Conscience and Career Collide," p. 49.
7. John A. Howard, as quoted in *Bits and Pieces*, February 1977, p. 10.
8. Comarow, "When Conscience and Career Collide," p. 49.
9. Warren G. Bennis, "The Sense of Morality," *Royal Bank Letter*, vol. 65, no. 1, January/February 1984 (Royal Bank of Canada).
10. *Management Review*, May 1977, p. 34.

Chapter Seven

HONESTY IN THE HOME

~

Since I began this study and started writing on honesty and ethics, I have been the object of considerable scrutiny by my children. Frequently, as I have been driving and the speed has crept over the legal limit, a voice comes over my shoulder from the back seat: "Ethics, Dad, ethics!"

I am increasingly aware that my children constantly watch and imitate me. Nothing I do is private. My children see me as I really am.

As I have contemplated this, I have sensed the extent of my responsibility to them as a father and as a model for their lives, both in actions and attitudes.

Scripture says, "Do not be deceived, God is not mocked; for whatever a man sows, this he will also reap" (Galatians 6:7). We experience this truth most fully in the home. What we sow in our homes and lives will be reaped in the lives of our children. But home presents an unfair arena, we may say. We are so vulnerable and observable there. After all, where else can we let our hair down and be ourselves? But that is just the point: Our true selves provide the pattern for our children to follow. If our faith is real, it must permeate even the privacy of the home. In fact, if it is not apparent in the home, is it real at all?

HONEST ACTIONS

"What you do speaks so loudly I can't hear what you say." This old saying reflects the view children have as they mature. They compare the standards they are taught with the standards by which their parents live. The parents' actions make a deep impression on children, which no amount of words can alter. Let us examine some areas in which this influence is strongest.

Taxes and Business Dealings

Will Rogers said, "The income tax has made more liars out of the American people than golf has."[1] Attempted cheating on income taxes has become common practice. Few people try to cheat in a major way, but they feel it is their right to get by with small deceptions.

Let's look at a possible example. John was well-known in his professional circles. He had been a Christian for several years and often was called to share his faith in religious meetings all around the United States. For this he often received honorariums. Early one April, after a hectic session with his accountant, he exploded at the dinner table in the presence of his wife and his college-age son.

"The Federal Government is the biggest rip-off artist in history! We're going to have to pay more income taxes this year than ever before. Well, I'm not going to tell anybody about the honorariums. Too bad. They can just miss out. They get plenty anyway!"

A few years later he was stunned and saddened when his son, who by then was established in a career, failed to pass an audit by the Internal Revenue Service, and was heavily fined for tax evasion. When John confronted his son, he received this response: "Who do you think taught me to cheat? You're the expert, Dad." John left his embittered son with a sick sense of guilt and loss.

You may say, "But my children wouldn't be aware of anything like that. In fact, they know nothing of my business dealings." Don't they? Think back on various conversations with your spouse when your children were nearby or in the next room. What about those questionable deductions you talked about? Consider not only how you ultimately decided to handle them, but the way in which you discussed them. Children hear our implications as well as our spoken words.

As your children become teenagers you may need to discuss with them their earnings and how that affects your income tax deductions. What will you say? And when they ask you for financial advice, how will you respond? Teenagers will quickly adopt your attitudes as you instruct them. And aside from the impact on your children, how does your financial conduct affect your own conscience? If you are not totally honest in paying your taxes, can you truly train your children in other areas of honesty?

Have you developed biblical convictions regarding your responsibility to the government? Have you discussed these biblical teachings with your children? You may wish to pursue further reading and study on this topic in these passages: Matthew 17:24-27, 22:16-22; Romans 13:1-7; and 1 Peter 2:13-17.

Often we think children are unaware of our business dealings. But their perception is much greater than we give them credit for. They observe whether we pay the paper carrier promptly, whether we tip fairly, and how we react to such things as being overcharged at a store. From these minor indicators they begin to develop their own convictions as well as forming an opinion of our honesty and fairness.

Since our job consumes so much of our lives, we often

discuss it at the dinner table or around the house. The boast about "getting away" with something at work or "making a killing" in some competitive sales opportunity filters into our children's minds and reveals our character. What about "sick leave"? The children see that you are perfectly well, yet perhaps you (or your spouse) call in sick in order to use the day for personal pursuits. Or they may see you include personal items on your expense account. Children, especially teenagers, understand these things.

We are also vulnerable to our children's scrutiny when we entertain business associates at home. The children may have previously heard us talk about these associates, and they compare our private discussion with how we now speak with them personally. If they observe contradictions, they will begin to regard us as hypocritical.

Obeying the Law

We daily live within the constraints of the laws of our nation and community. As children grow, they develop a keen sense of what is legally right and wrong, and their view of the law depends greatly on how they observe us relating to it.

For example, let's say that Reverend Mitchell pastored a sizable church in his community. He was greatly loved by his parishioners who tolerated and even joked about his one apparent fault—driving over the speed limit. After his son earned his driver's license, Reverend Mitchell was angry and disappointed when the boy had three auto accidents in his first six months of driving. After carefully reviewing the situation and recognizing his contribution to the boy's problem, Reverend Mitchell talked at length with his son and asked his forgiveness for the poor example he had given. The son responded well to his father's admission and neither of them received any traffic tickets or had any accidents after that time.

During the eighteen or so years a son or daughter lives

with us, they not only know our actions and responses, but they also adopt many of them. When our children see us violate traffic laws or the many other rules and laws that govern much of our daily activities, they begin to do the same—with both the rules we impose on them and the laws of the community.

We must set an example for our children that speaks far more clearly than words—we must live within the law.

LOVE

Actions and expressions of love make deep impressions on children and on all those who know us, and honesty in our love is crucial. Words are important because our children need to be told that we love them and that they are important to us. They also need to hear us verbally express our love for our mate. Children find security in the fact that their parents have a real love relationship.

Love also needs to be expressed physically. When I embrace or kiss my wife in front of our children there are comments of "There go the lovers again," or "Good grief!" But this demonstration of love actually gives them a further sense of security and sets a pattern for their future marriages. Furthermore, as adults we need this expression of love from our mate.

Even with verbal and physical expressions of love, real honesty in love occurs when actions match the expressions. Children *expect* parents to love them. Our actions toward them and our mate must be a true reflection of love.

Children perceive the reality of love from our actions and attitudes, and they assess the honesty of our love by our treatment of others. An outburst of anger and impatience at another driver, for example, can give a child more insight into our life than hours of lectures on Christian love. A few offhand comments about their lazy friends or the lower social status of a classmate's parents can also give them a glimpse into our true attitudes. Our treatment and acceptance of their friends is important to them. The way in which we speak to and about their friends demonstrates our love for our children.

Recently Mary and I returned from a trip and had an interesting surprise at home. My brother had hitchhiked into town the previous day. As he was waiting for my son, Steve, to pick him up at a local restaurant, he began talking to a teenage boy. He found that this boy had just run away from home with no place to go. It was a cold December night and he had only a light jacket and a thin blanket. For two nights he had tried to sleep outdoors, but the weather was so cold he couldn't sleep, so my brother invited him to our home. When we arrived, we found the young runaway living in our home. We were unsure of our legal responsibilities. We knew nothing about him or the truthfulness of his story, so naturally fears regarding the safety of our family raced through our minds. What should we do? Call his parents? The police? Send him away?

As I talked with him, I noticed that Steve intently listened to every word and watched me like a hawk. The boy was one year younger than Steve and I imagine Steve felt compassion for him. To Steve this situation was a test of my love and concern for others. We decided to let him stay. Two days later the boy wanted to return to his parents so we put him on a bus headed for his hometown. I believe my credibility in the area of honest love would have been seriously damaged in my son's eyes if I had not offered concern and help to this troubled teenager.

HONEST COMMUNICATION

The son of a pastor in a large western city took college entrance exams for admission to a prominent college. His scores were too low for admission, so he enlisted in the Air

Force. His father suggested that he tell people he had decided to get military service out of the way before going to college, implying that he could have gone to college but chose not to. The father also told others this story to shield the family from the embarrassment of failure. Later, while on active duty in the Air Force, the son encountered great spiritual difficulties and his life began to disintegrate. Perhaps much of his difficulty was related to this deception and other such examples from his parents. Such parental leadership could not help but produce guilt and problems of conscience.

Though you may never lie (or encourage your children to lie) in such a blatant way, consider how honest your communications really are. Do you faithfully keep your promises? Is your speech sprinkled with exaggerations and half-truths? Do you gossip? Do you admit your mistakes?

PROMISES

On my daughter's fifteenth birthday I promised her a ski trip to Aspen, Colorado where one of her favorite singers lived. But in the month and a half of ski season remaining we did not do it, although Kathy reminded me of it frequently. For the next summer and fall she reminded me of it at least once a month, always with the question of whether or not I would honor my promise next year. Soon a question of my honesty of intent was raised. The issue was not fully settled until we finally made a ski trip (though it was to an area closer to home).

Promises mean a lot to children. No matter how small the promised thing may be, the words, "But Dad, you promised!" reveal the intensity of feeling and expectation in the heart of a child. Children don't understand idle promises or offhand statements.

As parents, we constantly insist that our children meet their promises to us. Is it unusual that they would expect us to reciprocate and carry out our promises? If they cannot trust us in these small personal interactions with them, how can we expect them to believe us when we try to teach them spiritual truths and moral values?

But promises are important not only to children. Our spouse also wants desperately to believe that we will fulfill our promises to them. I am not always a punctual person. Frequently I will cram far more into a day than I should, and, consequently, find myself tardy for certain things. Often I say that I will be back at a certain time. And often I do not make it. This not only irritates my wife, but shatters her faith in my time commitments. I have improved and she has become more tolerant, but I still live with this reputation with my wife. Certainly this has caused needless conflict in our relationship. Even though I do not *intend* to break a promise, it happens. I have had to either stop predicting my arrival or make sure that I can be there. It is simply a matter of courtesy and honesty to fulfill my word to her.

Do you make promises to your mate that you don't or cannot keep? Your word is far more important than you may realize. If you cannot keep promises, do not make them. At the same time, you should not avoid all promises and commitments simply to free yourself from the possibility of failure.

Gossip

One of the most damaging kinds of dishonest communication is gossip. Gossip occurs in two ways—when we speak that which is untrue or hearsay, and when we speak the truth but violate a private communication or confidentiality.

In our home, our talk about other people has a profound effect on our children and our mate. A daughter who hears her mother griping frequently on the phone to a friend will soon begin doing it herself. A son who hears his father criticize someone will begin to develop the same attitude. Then, as children grow older and realize that much of what we have said is untrue, they will lose respect for us and our opinions.

Children are great at jumping to conclusions on the barest of facts, exaggerating beyond the limits of reality, and being judgmental toward others. Most adults can recognize when children make these rash judgments and so we begin to challenge their accuracy and to moderate their attitudes. But how can we honestly correct our children when we do the same thing—although in a far more sophisticated and veiled manner? We must not be deceived into thinking that children cannot see this disparity. Paul, writing to Christians at Ephesus, gave us the proper guidelines: "Let no unwholesome word proceed from your mouth, but only such a word as is good for edification according to the need of the moment, that it may give grace to those who hear" (Ephesians 4:29).

APOLOGIES

One of the greatest things that can happen in a home is for a parent to admit he is wrong and to apologize and ask forgiveness of a son or daughter. As my daughter Karen often says when confronted with some issue, "Well, nobody is perfect!" Right. No one is perfect, but few will admit to their faults. When you have spoken to your son or daughter in anger or accused them unjustly, have you ever apologized to them and asked their forgiveness? You must if you want to have honest communications in your home. If you demand confession and apologies from them, should they not expect it from you?

A friend of mine and I were driving in a car with one of his children. As we were discussing the book Mary and I had written on work, his son asked him, "Dad, have you read this book?" He replied that he had only read part of it. A month later he called me to confess that this was not true.

He said he really had not read it, but to impress me had made a false statement. His conscience allowed no rest until he corrected the situation with both his son and me. Can you imagine the impact this apology had on his son? Rather than causing him to disrespect his father, I believe it served to deepen their relationship and to demonstrate genuine honesty.

Have you ever apologized to one of your children for something? If not, you may need to recall three or four incidents of the past for which you need to ask their forgiveness. As difficult as this may be (especially if they are teenagers or adults), it may be the necessary action to begin the process of developing the close relationship you always longed for with your children. You may also need to do the same thing with your husband or wife.

We desperately need this honest communication, because it is the foundation for truly close relationships.

DEVELOPING HONESTY IN CHILDREN

Children possess a keen sense of justice and fairness, as well as honesty. Every parent has repeatedly heard the cry, "That's not fair!" Children notice who gets the biggest piece of cake, whose Christmas present is largest, whose allowance was increased. They also notice if we or others deal honestly with them in each interaction. Whether our action truly is honest, fair, or just does not always matter, but what they *think* is honest, fair, and just burns deeply on their minds and consciences.

A child's plea for honesty rests securely in the intent of the oath, "Cross your heart and hope to die, stick a needle in your eye." Children want truth and honesty in all their relationships, for this gives them the security of knowing they can trust people. When this trust is violated, they develop suspicions that disturb their concept of truth—

especially when the person in question is a trusted authority such as a parent or a teacher.

When my daughter Karen was thirteen, I took her and her best friend to a concert by one of her favorite singers. Since the concert was held sixty miles away, she planned the entire outing far in advance, thinking of every detail from driving time to standing-in-line time. She talked of it daily with the keen anticipation that most adults can only remember from childhood. We planned to leave three and a half hours early, stop at McDonald's for dinner, drive to the parking lot of the large basketball arena, get in line at the doors, and still have thirty minutes to find our seats.

After we arrived, we waited with several thousand teenage girls who wriggled in their seats, giggling in anticipation of seeing the star in person. Finally, the dimming of the lights drew deafening squeals of delight from the crowd. Then the spotlight shot at the stage and four teenage singers began their gyrations. Karen squinted through our binoculars and asked, "But, where is . . . ?" The star wasn't there. But surely he would be soon, they said. Fifteen minutes went by and the other singers continued on stage. Still no star. Thirty minutes. Kids started chanting for him to come out. Karen and her friend were becoming angry. "That's a gyp. We paid $8.25 for this and all we get are these dumb guys!" As the minutes ticked into three-quarters of an hour, their irritation and disappointment grew. They were offended. It just wasn't fair.

Finally the star came. He sang and the audience screamed and clapped. Forty-five minutes later he bounded off the stage surrounded by his bodyguards, and it was over.

The trip was a success. Score one for Dad's friendship with Karen. But in every description of the event, one detail always received notice. The first half was a gyp. It was unfair. They came to see the star, and he wasn't there.

Not having attended one of these concerts before, Karen

and her friend had not realized that most concerts have an opening act. But that didn't matter to them. Their sense of fairness and justice had been offended, and the incident would be remembered for years. They felt deceived.

God gives children their deep-seated sense of justice and fairness. But this sense can either develop or decay. Parents must do everything possible to use this God-given sense to develop a deep commitment to honesty. "Train up a child in the way he should go (and in keeping with his individual gift or bent), and when he is old he will not depart from it" (Proverbs 22:6, AMP). A child has a bent to fairness and honesty that we can expand and activate. But how can we do this in a purposeful way?

TYPICAL PROBLEMS OF DISHONESTY

Lying constitutes the most common abuse of honesty in children. They may lie about something wrong they think they have done, or an act of disobedience they have deliberately committed. Lying is a defense mechanism to avoid punishment or gain acceptance. As a child moves beyond preschool years, lying can develop into a mode of life if the parents have not established firm guidelines for truth in the home. In the teen years dishonesty can become purposeful deceit.

Cheating among children often appears early in their lives when they cheat in sports or games in order to win. Again, the concepts developed early in life lay the foundation for cheating or honesty later. But peer pressure strongly challenges even the best home training. Cheating in school has become so common that it may be the norm for many children. Cheating provides a simple way to achieve and succeed without working hard.

Early training provides the best protection against cheating. Open communication and sound biblical teaching can restore proper attitudes about cheating in older children and teenagers.

Stealing, more than lying or cheating, hurts other people. When one of our daughters was three years old, she took a large colorful bubble gum ball from the candy shelf of a local store. When her mother noticed it in the car, they had a long talk and then returned to the store where our daughter apologized to the clerk and replaced the ball. Fortunately it was wrapped in cellophane! The clerk responded properly by thanking our daughter and urging her never again to take anything from anyone unless she first asked permission or paid. Our daughter may have been a little young to grasp all the implications involved in the incident, but to our knowledge she has never again stolen anything.

Children steal to get something they want. Early in life they form attitudes toward other people's property. If a child gets away with stealing at this stage, he soon regards stealing as an easy way to acquire things.

Only rarely is stealing related to material needs, but rather with wants and desires. For some children, stealing brings attention from parents who neglected them earlier. Other children have lost their sense of right and believe that stealing is not wrong unless they get caught. These patterns begun in childhood continue in adolescence and adulthood.

CAUSES OF DISHONESTY

Dishonesty stems from many roots, but five major causes stand out.

1. *Fear* drives children, teenagers, and adults to lie, cheat, and steal. Just as fear of failure causes adults to say things that are untrue, fear of punishment tempts children to lie to escape the consequences of wrong actions. Memories of discipline unjustly or unwisely administered implant real fright in their hearts and minds, and lying presents the easiest escape. Later, lying to cover up mistakes becomes a way of life. But the root cause, even for adults, is fear: fear

of discovery, fear of the truth, fear of punishment, fear of losing a job, and fear of broken pride and losing face.

One who has never experienced the paralysis of fear cannot imagine its power over the mind and the will. A parent who indiscriminately hits or spanks a child knows the panic glance of fear that leaps into a child's eyes with even the raising of the hand. The memory of past blows awakens a fear that will make a child say almost anything to avoid another barrage of punishment.

2. *Lack of teaching* in the home produces children who do not know what is right and wrong. Some parents take no personal responsibility for teaching and training their children, leaving it all to society and the schools. This problem multiplies when the parents themselves do not possess deep moral convictions.

3. *Parental example* teaches what no amount of words can communicate. A PTA announcement was sent out to all parents asking them to come to a special meeting. They were asked to bring all their towels from motels and hotels all over the world. When they came, they were hung up in rows across the front — from Hong Kong, Japan, Germany, and all major hotel chains. The speaker then announced the topic — "How to Teach Your Children Honesty." No one picked up their towels after the meeting!

If parents act dishonestly or treat their children in a dishonest manner, the inevitable result will be dishonest children. The example of brothers and sisters, as well as his own circle of friends, also influences a child's values and molds his moral fiber.

4. *Greed* drives people to act in ways they once thought impossible. The thirst for material possessions and the aversion to honest work combine to drive people to dishonesty, keeping this temptation in the forefront of the mind. Children raised in a materialistic home where greed is open and unchecked later have difficulty living within their means,

and feel they deserve what they desire no matter how they obtain it.

5. In rare instances, true *psychological problems* underlie dishonest behavior. When this occurs, professional help from a trusted pastor or a qualified counselor should be sought. Pathological or compulsive lying or stealing differs significantly from typical childhood dishonesty—both in frequency and in the child's ability to change. If you suspect this problem in your child, seek professional help immediately.

DEVELOPING HONESTY IN CHILDREN

Most parents would rather train than correct—but few do it. By the time we see the need for training, we are already in the corrective phase. But if we commit ourselves to preventive and developmental training when children are small, we can avoid months and years of grief and strain.

Training takes time, effort, and foresight. It also requires a parent to develop his own convictions. We cannot communicate something we have not thought and prayed about. Here are some suggestions on the training process of developing honesty in a child.

1. *Lead your child to Christ.* No amount of training can replace the proper foundation in life. Jesus' story of the wise man and the foolish man (Matthew 7:24-27) gives us keen insight. The foolish man built his house on the sand and it was destroyed by the rains and storms. The wise man did his building on a rock, and his house stood. Jesus Christ provides the only foundation for building true character. We cannot instill concepts of honesty in our children without the foundation of salvation. We must constantly expose them to the gospel and pray that they will understand it and receive Christ early in life.

One of the greatest experiences parents can have is to personally lead their children to Christ. From then on we always have the reference point of Scripture and God's design for them as the basis of our teaching. If we begin experiencing serious problems of dishonesty with our children, we need to make sure they have truly made a personal decision to become a Christian.

2. *Teach them Bible principles.* When children are young we can force outward obedience and conformity. As they grow older, their true response to commands and requests must come from their inner life. If they are Christians, the most powerful and controlling force is the inner conviction implanted by the Word of God and activated by the Spirit of God. Human principles will not suffice. Only Bible principles possess life-changing ability.

From the earliest ages our children need to begin learning principles of conduct and honesty from the Bible, and we must answer their questions in these areas with biblical truth. They can learn biblical guidelines from the stories of such Bible characters as the good Samaritan (Luke 10:25-37), Ananias and Sapphira (Acts 5:1-11), Philemon and Onesimus (Philemon), David and Saul (1 Samuel 24), and Joseph (Genesis 39–41).

Memorizing Scripture also imparts biblical principles. Children can begin with salvation verses such as John 3:16; Romans 3:23, 5:8, 6:23; Ephesians 2:8-9. Then they can move to character verses such as Luke 10:27, Romans 12:17, and Ephesians 4:29,32. The Scripture will accomplish a work in their lives that parents can never do. "The Word of God is living and active and sharper than any two-edged sword, and piercing as far as the division of soul and spirit, of both joints and marrow, and able to judge the thoughts and intentions of the heart" (Hebrews 4:12).

3. *Maintain a good personal example.* Next to the Word of God, your conduct as a parent can be the best influence in forming the character of your children. They imitate you far more than you expect. Have you ever met a young person and wondered why he acted, talked, and thought in a

particular manner? Then when you met his mother or father you probably saw the same kinds of actions, speech, or thoughts. The prospect of our influence almost frightens us. The power of our example is overwhelming. Children become what we are. Therefore, we must make certain our lives are proper examples of honesty.

4. *Practice consistent discipline.* In the complex process of training children, discipline cannot be neglected. Lying, cheating, and stealing deserve punishment of some kind. However, effective discipline demands consistency, compassion, and careful thought. Most children sense the magnitude of their offenses and know the risk of punishment. But they have a keen sense of justice and fairness. They expect a just measure of discipline when caught. If discipline is excessively harsh or ridiculously light we risk making them bitter or encouraging further breaches of conduct. Our discipline must be based on compassion and concern, not ignorance or inconsistency. Discipline must fit the offense, the age of the child, the particular circumstance, and the child's response to the situation.[2]

5. *Reward and encourage honesty.* Positive reinforcement of honest actions far outweighs punishment of dishonesty in having a lasting effect in a child's life. We must seize every opportunity to commend honesty at any level. We all respond to compliments and encouragement, and children especially do this. They will be honest if we let them know their honesty pleases us. So often we clearly let them know what displeases us, but are silent when they do well. They need clear verbal feedback. We need to tell them we appreciate what they do, especially when they are honest to their disadvantage.

At times their honesty may even result in punishment. When children admit their wrong actions honestly, we may indeed need to punish them. Their sense of justice and fairness tells them they deserve it. However, because they honestly admitted their mistakes, we ought to lessen or at times eliminate punishment as a reward for honesty.

In teaching honesty in the home, one missing element may particularly destroy any opportunity to influence your children. This missing element is personal humility before your children and mate, and the willingness to admit you are wrong. As mentioned earlier, it is important to admit mistakes or apologize to children. One of the most influential things you can do for your children is to say, "Son, do you remember what I said the other day about why I couldn't take you to the ball game? Well, I lied to you. I could have done it. Will you forgive me?" The impact of that confession will do more to teach and train your children than any amount of theoretical teaching. Many times I have had to confess anger or ask my children's forgiveness for being unjustly harsh to them. It was not easy. The most difficult five words in the English language are "I'm sorry. Please forgive me." Do you need to make some confession to your mate or children? Do it now. This is the first step toward restoring any relationship.

CONFRONTING AND HANDLING DISHONESTY
In spite of teaching and training, children are at times dishonest. How we respond to their dishonesty is crucial. Handled properly, the situation can foster confidence and effective training. Handled wrongly, it can make our children bitter and distrustful. A wise parent plans his strategy *before* a problem occurs. Here are a few ideas on what to do.

1. *Know the facts.* Unjust accusations and punishment damage our credibility with our children. Let's think through a possible example. Stan drove into his driveway after a day of hard work and extra pressure on the job. He breathed a sigh of relief as he switched off the motor. Now he could relax. Just as he entered the front door of the house, his five-year-old daughter Marcia ran into his arms

sobbing, "Rick kicked me and scratched me!" He saw some long scratches on her arms, and she screamed as he touched her leg. Anger welled up inside him and he ran up two steps at a time to his seven-year-old son's room.

"All right, Rick, what's the idea of treating your sister that way?"

"Dad, I didn't. . . ."

"What do you mean you didn't?" Stan interrupted. "I saw those scratches and the bruise. Did you do that?"

"Yes, but. . . ."

"But nothing! You're going to be punished. We don't allow that sort of thing at our house."

Stan spanked him soundly and left Rick crying in his room.

As he went back downstairs his wife asked what was happening. He told her the situation and saw a puzzled look in her eyes. She said she had overheard part of the altercation and wondered if he had all the facts. He got both of the children together and found that the scratches were not deliberate but accidental, and that Marcia had first grabbed a handful of Rick's hair. He felt sick as he realized he had jumped to a conclusion and could not take back the spanking. He asked Rick to forgive him and apologized for not listening. Then he had to punish Marcia.

Frequently we act without knowing all the facts. Whenever you suspect dishonesty, be certain you really know what happened. If your child is generally honest with you, it may be possible to simply ask for the facts and share your concern. Above all, do not jump to conclusions on skimpy information. Hear the child with patience and understanding.

2. *Pray*. Before you take any specific action, pray. This is particularly essential when facts are incomplete and you cannot determine if the child was dishonest in some way. When you are trying to determine appropriate punishment or training, you must rely on God for insight. God is more

interested in a child's personal and spiritual development than any parent. We desperately need insight from Him and His Word. "If any of you lacks wisdom, let him ask of God, who gives to all men generously and without reproach, and it will be given to him" (James 1:5). And when are we more dependent on God's wisdom than in training our children? Pray in every circumstance and for each child, because each circumstance and each child is unique and deserves special consideration.

3. *Give them opportunity to confess and explain.* Correction frequently consists of simply punishing an act rather than preventing further wrongdoing. We must focus our correction on building into the child's inner person the will and desire to do the right thing, and punishment may not contribute to that goal.

For more enduring correction, confession and repentance are two of the most important concepts for a child to learn when he has sinned. Confession should be to God and to the parent. Children need to learn that sin breaks relationships with both God and man, and confession restores the relationship. "If we confess our sins, He is faithful and righteous to forgive us our sins and to cleanse us from all unrighteousness" (1 John 1:9).

Learn to ask gentle questions that do not assume guilt. "How do you feel about what you told Dad this afternoon?" "Did some other things happen this afternoon that you thought of after we talked?" "You look a little unhappy. Is anything bothering you?" When children admit guilt, especially in cheating or stealing, stimulate them to express how they feel inside: "I know you feel bad about that. Would you like to talk about it?" "I know you were upset and scared when we talked earlier. How do you feel now?"

At times, forcefulness and direct pressure may be needed, but such occasions should be rare. In encounters with my children, I sometimes approached them like a prosecuting attorney. But that was unfair. Children need the love of a parent, not the accusations of a lawyer.

The Word of God, the Holy Spirit, and their conscience are the instruments God uses to convict children of wrongdoing. But the development of these aspects of life takes time. We must be patient, pray, and wait for God to work in our child's heart. In this delicate and sensitive area of honesty, true character cannot be developed in a brief incident of punishment. We must allow God to work in His time, and to use us in the process.

In addition to confession, many children need the opportunity to explain why they acted as they did. We are usually too quick to blurt out, "I don't want excuses. Just tell me the truth." But we may learn far more about the inner thoughts of our son or daughter by carefully hearing them out. And we must hear them out—without impolite interruptions. In line with their sense of justice and fairness, they feel deeply that they deserve an honest hearing. With older children, it is often best to listen first, and not respond fully until an hour or two later—or even the next day. Even as I write this I feel a pang in my heart, and wish I had more carefully followed this advice.

"A brother offended is harder to be won than a strong city" (Proverbs 18:19). Spiritually, our children are our brothers and sisters, and they do get offended. It may take a lifetime to win them back.

4. *Confront the issue, not just the act.* Since our purpose is not to accuse but to change, we need to discern motives as well as actions. Actions are seen, but motives are discerned. *Why* a child or teenager lied or cheated or stole is more important than the act. Was it from fear, peer pressure, greed, laziness, or rebellion? It may take several instances to give you insight on motives. When you punish or confront only the act, remember that you have not yet dealt with the real issue.

5. *Punish when punishment is due*. In a stealing incident similar to the one our daughter experienced, the mother returned to the store and sought out the manager. She explained to him what had happened. He saw the tears on the girl's face as she handed back some candy to him and he said, "Oh, that's all right. Don't worry about it." As the mother began to protest, he insisted that it was no problem. Finally she said to the manager, "Please don't say that it is all right. It is not. She stole it and I am trying to teach her that it is wrong."

Punishment and restitution must be part of the training process for all ages. Occasionally punishment may consist of a strong discussion and verbal chastisement. But frequently for younger children the punishment must be physical. Older children may be helped most by a deprivation of their privileges. Making restitution is often one of the most effective punishments for cheating or stealing. Restitution can be embarrassing and humiliating, but it makes a memorable impression.

But whatever form is used, parents must realize the necessity of punishment. "Because the sentence against an evil deed is not executed quickly, therefore the hearts of the sons of men among them are given fully to do evil" (Ecclesiastes 8:11). Here are a few guidelines for applying punishment:

- Make the punishment fit the crime. Don't overpunish for small misdeeds.
- Be as consistent as you can in dealing with each issue. Punishment one time and not the next confuses a child.
- In corporal punishment (spanking) be careful not to hurt the child, or to spank for every little thing. As a child grows older, you must rely more and more on persuasion and influence.

- Never punish when you are angry.
- Be consistent with all the children in the family.
- Punishment, both physical and verbal, should be in private. Public correction humiliates and angers a child.
- Assure the child of your love in the process.
- Be certain the child understands why he is being punished.

6. *Forgive and reassure them.* Children (and adults) need to know they have been forgiven. We cannot live under the burden of unforgiven offenses. Both younger children and teenagers need reassurance of love and confidence from parents. They also need to know that parents do not bear a grudge against them.

When our son, Steve, was in the sixth grade I received a note from his school principal saying Steve had been reported saying certain swear words to another child. I talked to Steve and, as he always did, he honestly admitted what he had said. After some serious discussion about it, I let him know that it was over and forgotten. Yet the note was a very condemning thing to have. I thought of how he could imagine me keeping it and holding it over his head later. So Steve and I went to the kitchen sink, and I took a match and set the note on fire. The ashes in the sink provided a visual emphasis that the incident was done, forgiven, and forgotten. It never occurred again.

Use every opportunity to teach and train. Certainly, confronting and handling dishonesty provides a unique opportunity for teaching by a godly, concerned parent. Do not abandon one of the most significant opportunities God has given you as a parent.

"Fathers, do not provoke your children to anger; but bring them up in the discipline and instruction of the Lord" (Ephesians 6:4).

Notes
1. Will Rogers, as quoted in *Bits and Pieces*, September 1976, p. 1.
2. On the subject of disciplining children I recommend *The New Dare to Discipline* by James Dobson (Wheaton, Ill.: Tyndale, 1970, 1992).

Chapter Eight

HONESTY AS A STUDENT

———————— ∾ ————————

The chatter in the room dwindled to a few nervous comments and jokes as the professor began passing out the exams. Several students hastily reviewed their notes. Others sat nervously tapping their pencils on the desks. The normal pre-exam tension filled the air, accompanied by sweaty palms and jittery stomachs.

The professor gave a few brief words of explanation and walked out of the room, leaving two student proctors to monitor the exam and answer questions. There was a rustle of relief as soon as he left. Crib sheets emerged, books opened, and dozens of students began cheating blatantly.

One student, however, saw the obvious cheating and became inwardly agitated. A former cadet at the United States Air Force Academy, he was now working on a special assignment to complete his master's degree. He had been trained for four years under an honor code at the academy.

Finally, he stood up and announced to the class, "What you people are doing is wrong! It is cheating! I can't stand for it and I plan to report this to the instructor!"

He sat down as abruptly as he had stood. The class was speechless. Then a new wave of nervousness swept over the room.

After the exam several students congratulated the student for his courage. Cheating bothered them too, they said, but it was so common they had felt unable to do anything.

The student reported the cheating, and the exams were discarded and a new test was administered. What was accomplished by his action? It didn't stop all the cheating, but a clear standard of right was established in the class. Others were given courage to act on their convictions in the future, and the student himself had a strengthened sense of integrity and the peace of a clear conscience.

Cheating on all academic levels has become so common that even some parents and teachers no longer show concern. And honest students face increasing pressure to conform to the trend. *Newsweek* magazine reported that a survey at Stanford University showed that 45 percent of the student body "had committed at least one act of serious cheating such as plagiarism." The article quoted one dean at the University of Wisconsin, who handled 150 cases of academic misconduct reported to him each year, as saying, "If what I hear is true, that doesn't even scratch the tip of the iceberg."[1]

I served for six years on the faculty of the United States Air Force Academy. Students there, as well as at the United States Military Academy at West Point, must ascribe to an honor code which states, "I will not lie, cheat, or steal, nor tolerate those who do." There have always been "cheating scandals" at these and other institutions where honor codes exist. But highly publicized incidents in recent years seemed to particularly touch off a flurry of protests against the codes, especially the "toleration" clause. "Ratting" on a friend offends some people's sense of justice. The real issue, however, is whether it is acceptable to "lie, cheat, or steal" if we do not get caught.

Two of these "cheating scandals" at the Air Force Academy occurred while I was a professor there, and I made a few observations. The problems arose because we have attempted to impose a Christian ethic on an essentially nonChristian society.

The academies have not changed appreciably—but the incoming students have. They are the product of a society where biblical standards of honor and moral integrity do not command respect. The Christian ethical influence in our society has been reduced considerably in recent years, and persons from a social environment where cheating is accepted cannot change overnight simply by mental assent to an honor code.

The near impossibility of imposing a biblical standard of honesty on a society that does not hold the Judeo-Christian foundation it once had was recognized in a West Point study.[2] This study described the academy's honor code as "a clear and simple statement of an unattainable level of human behavior." But the study also quoted one graduate of West Point as saying, "Of course, the reconciliation of an absolute code with an imperfect world requires considerable judgment. But it remains the fundamental assumption of the West Point honor code that only deep respect for those absolute principles of honesty can prepare men to make those judgments. In short, men must know the absolute principles of honesty in order to apply them situationally in the 'real world.' These absolute principles are embodied in the cadet honor code. . . . The development of judgment in the application of honor runs throughout the maintenance of the honor code and system at West Point." The authors of the study agreed: "The idealistic U.S.M.A. honor code deserves to be retained, but it must be recognized as a goal rather than an actuality."

But for the believer the existence of an imperfect—or even immoral—society can never be an excuse for cheating.

One of the central truths of the Bible is that the Christian is surrounded by forces that push him to conform, but that he must obey God no matter what the cost or consequences. "Do not love the world," the apostle John wrote. "The world is passing away, and also its lusts; but the one who does the will of God abides forever" (1 John 2:15,17).

The Christian lives under a different moral order than the world around him—God's. The Old Testament laws regarding cheating and stealing are reinforced in the New Testament by Christ's law of love and by specific instructions for honest conduct.

How should believing students withstand the pressures and the temptations to cheat? It is not enough to simply say, "Don't cheat." To develop personal convictions in this area we need to understand the motives for cheating as well as reasons for not cheating.

WHY STUDENTS CHEAT

People do not cheat because they think it is right. In fact, most people instinctively know it is wrong. They do not even want to cheat—but they do. Why?

THE PRESSURE OF SOCIETY

In a society where even our leaders lie and cheat, it is no wonder that students ignore teaching against cheating. No observant young person can miss the hypocrisy, in public and in private, of many of our leaders. Their example teaches what no measure of instruction can overcome.

Television programs also feature heroes who lie and cheat to obtain their ends. I remember a night when I sat down to relax by watching a new comedy program in which the star was a good-looking, young detective. I laughed along with the program until I began noticing that in every interview with people the detective lied to obtain his information. The program was teaching that the end justifies the means, and cleverly concealed this wrong teaching in a humorous cloak.

As a young person sees his parents, leaders, and other adults acting out this kind of philosophy, he soon begins to act it out himself. Society effectively brainwashes the student, and he does not see that cheating will eventually be self-defeating.

THE PRESSURE OF GRADES AND PERFORMANCE

We live in a world oriented to production and performance. We are judged by what we do, not by who we are. We gain acceptance by how well we perform and how much we produce. Grades are the major indicator of a student's performance. So if grades determine his worth, he may well think that any means of getting them is justified.

Most of us can identify with this pressure. And even though I understand it, I still give an inordinate amount of attention to the grades my children receive in school rather than checking on what they are really learning and what is being taught in their classrooms. Most parents of teenagers seem to relax as long as their children receive acceptable grades and avoid using drugs.

Grades are important as a measure of learning — but not all-important. Parents need to develop a healthy perspective on grades and to relieve the pressure on our children to overachieve.

Intensifying this pressure for older students is the fact that competition for entry into college graduate schools increases every year, especially for medical, dental, and law schools. Students can become so obsessed with getting A's to obtain further graduate education that they feel strong pressure to cheat — especially if others do. This pressure can be overcome by honest work and a proper perspective on education.

LAZINESS

In many cases, students cheat simply out of laziness. They want the diploma, but they don't want to work for it. "After all," they may say, "there is a lot more to college than study." So, to avoid the hard work of study and still pass their courses, they cheat.

Laziness is clearly warned against in Scripture. Solomon wrote, "I walked by the field of a certain lazy fellow and saw that it was overgrown with thorns, and covered with weeds; and its walls were broken down. Then, as I looked, I learned this lesson: 'A little extra sleep, a little more slumber, a little folding of the hands to rest' means that poverty will break in upon you suddenly like a robber, and violently like a bandit" (Proverbs 24:30-34, TLB).

Cheating compounds the sin of laziness. Its result will be failure and the lack of God's blessing.

PEER PRESSURE

Perhaps stronger than the general pressure of society, and the pressure of performance, is the pressure to cheat which students receive from their peers. Most students do not begin school with a master plan for cheating. Rather, it just happens. As others cheat and ridicule the honest student, and as pressures build and circumstances become adverse, he also cheats one time, and a pattern is started—not by design, but by his not recognizing and withstanding the pressure.

OVERCOMING FAILURE

Fear of failure may be the strongest factor in driving people to violate their conscience and compromise their standards. Failure is a fact of life. It is not a matter of *if* we fail, but *when* we fail. And no failure is pleasant. Failure is hard, humbling, and costly. But failure is not final; rather, it is part of a delicate process of growth and development in our lives.

Great success is often preceded by great failure. As a boy, Albert Einstein was so slow to talk that his parents thought him abnormal. His teachers called him a misfit and his classmates avoided him. He failed his first college entrance examination.[3] But he eventually became the world's most eminent scientist.

In the classroom, failure is despised and success is exalted. But a healthy view of failure helps a student to avoid cheating when the pressure is high.

When you fail, take the following steps.

1. *Take responsibility for the failure.* Do not blame the system, the boss, the professor, or anyone else. Accept personal responsibility. Admit that you have failed and go on from there.

2. *Analyze why you failed.* Many respond to failure by an emotional tailspin. Instead of harboring self-pity, analyze why you failed. Was it lack of discipline? A simple mistake? Lack of ability? Write down all the facts and come to reasonable conclusions.

3. *Look forward, not backward.* Don't live in the past. Learn from it, but don't live in it. The inventor Charles Kettering said, "My interest is in the future because I am going to spend the rest of my life there."[4] Learn all you can from your failure and then plan for the future. Paul said, "One thing I do: forgetting what lies behind and reaching forward to what lies ahead, I press on toward the goal for the prize of the upward call of God in Christ Jesus" (Philippians 3:13-14).

4. *Remember that God is sovereign.* When you fail, you may experience the temptation to doubt God's goodness. But God in His sovereignty always acts on our behalf. Even though you can

> see nothing in a failure that is your fault, be
> assured that God is at work in your life to deepen
> your character and to lead you in His perfect will.

When I first entered the Air Force my goal was to become a pilot. I had nearly completed pilot training and was doing well. Suddenly I failed a check ride in jet formation flying, and within days I was out of the program—with no second chance. I had failed. My pride was hurt, my ego was wounded, and I was puzzled by the whole thing. Yet I knew God was in charge and would lead me.

Later, though totally unrequested, I received an assignment to Cape Canaveral and became involved in the space program. The entire direction of my life and career was changed as a result of failure.

Looking back I can see God's perfect direction. I had personal needs and God was trying to get my attention. In His sovereignty, He redirected me to a future and a career I had never dreamed of.

But it began with failure!

In the Old Testament we see how Joseph's adult life began with years of apparent failure, but he later knew great success and honor (see Genesis 37, 39–41). Moses, too, failed the first time he tried to lead Israel (Exodus 5). Ilka Chase said, "The only people who never fail are those who never try."[5]

Again, Charles Kettering said, "All research is 99 percent failure, and if you succeed once you are in. If we are going to progress in any line, we must learn to fail intelligently, so we won't become discouraged at the 99 percent failures."[6]

Failure proves more beneficial than success gained by cheating and deceit. You may miss the greatest lessons of your life by cheating to avoid failure.

REASONS NOT TO CHEAT

CHEATING VIOLATES BIBLICAL COMMANDS

The foremost reason to avoid cheating is that it violates the commands of Scripture. When a student cheats, he implies that the exam he took or the term paper he wrote or the project he completed was entirely his work, done under stipulated rules. Thus, cheating is a direct form of lying, which Scripture forbids (see Colossians 3:9).

The Bible also provides examples of the consequences of cheating. In the New Testament church in Jerusalem, Ananias and Sapphira cheated by giving the impression they had contributed all the proceeds of the property they had sold. When confronted, both dropped dead as a result of their deception (Acts 5:1-11).

As a young man, Jacob cheated his brother out of his inheritance and deceived his father (Genesis 27). Later in Jacob's own family, his favorite wife was jealous (30:1); his favorite son was hated by his other sons (37:3-4) who then sold him to foreigners, bringing much sadness to Jacob (37:34); and he ultimately led Israel into its eventual slavery in Egypt (Genesis 46). God blessed Jacob because of His covenant with him, but Jacob clearly led a mostly miserable life. Cheating does not pay.

We can also place academic cheating under the biblical statements against deceit (Ephesians 4:22), falsehood (Proverbs 20:17, Ephesians 4:25), and stealing by unethically usurping someone else's position in a grading system. The specific category depends on the circumstances of the act.

CHEATING IS WARNED AGAINST BY OUR CONSCIENCE

Our conscience accuses us when we cheat, and unless we admit that the action was wrong, the conscience will become seared as the cheating occurs again and again. But then, even as believers, our conscience attempts to reach our will, and we cannot find peace.

The will and the conscience need development in "small" cheating matters to protect us from the larger issues of cheating. If we cheat as a student, we will build a bridge to cheating later in other areas of life — marriage, work, friendships, and our personal relationship with God.

Cheating Damages Our Personal Integrity and Trust

Beyond one's personal salvation, few things carry more value and vitality than personal integrity and trustworthiness. These qualities cannot be bought, and it will be said of the person who has them, "He can be trusted. He is a man of his word. He will do what is right. He will not cheat." They speak of wholeness of person and purpose. A person of integrity needs no collateral. He is like Nathaniel, in whom Jesus said there was no guile (John 1:47).

When personal integrity is lost, years must be spent rebuilding it. Christians who have lost their reputation for integrity are legion — and frequently they started with small indiscretions and impulsive actions. Most of them probably would have immediately overcome such temptations then if they had recognized the long-term consequences of such small acts.

Even though an act of cheating on our part may not be discovered by others, we know it ourselves, and personal integrity begins with personal self-respect. We must ask ourselves, "Knowing myself as well as I do, would I trust a person just like me?" What we are in private, that which others seldom see, is our real self.

Do not destroy in a moment of weakness that which takes years to rebuild. A reputation of personal integrity will serve you longer and better than any results obtained by cheating, and, moreover, you will be able to live at peace with yourself. Risking all this on so small a thing as an exam or course grade is sheer folly.

CHEATING ESTABLISHES WRONG HABITS

Our habits and lifestyle later in life change little from the formative years of high school and college. If, as a student, you choose to beat the system, defy codes of conduct, and violate rules, you will likely follow the same pattern later in your profession and family.

Present moral actions will persist later. Habits formed as a student will last a lifetime. If you cheat on exams, you will eventually cheat your company, your wife, your children, and your friends. Habits do not die quickly. Patterns of life and work remain constant through most of a person's adult life. Therefore, the wrong habits and patterns you establish in the first years of adulthood will likely continue—until you get caught or fail.

Paul said that those qualified for spiritual leadership should be "above reproach . . . [having] a good reputation with those outside the church," and that they should not be "double-tongued" (1 Timothy 3:2-8). Certainly cheating causes a person to fail these criteria. Students should guard their reputations jealously, building them with right habits and godly patterns of life.

CHEATING DEFEATS THE PURPOSE OF EDUCATION

We all agree that exam results and course grades do not entirely reflect true learning. Some educators would even say they defeat learning. But whether or not exams and the traditional grading system are valuable, cheating on them will certainly not enhance learning. If anything, it destroys the purpose of testing—the sampling of the knowledge a person should possess in a particular discipline.

The goal of a student is to learn. The goal of exams and grades is to measure learning. Therefore learning, not grades, should be the objective of a student. We may campaign for better teaching, fairer exams, and other reforms, but we must do so honestly in a constructive way. Cheating in any form cannot make education better. It is destructive and self-serving.

The nonbeliever may say that by cheating he is simply sidestepping an unfair system to reach his personal goals. But the believer cannot do this. He or she must seek higher goals, and must cling to honest methods to maintain his testimony and to influence society and the educational system.

HOW TO KEEP FROM CHEATING

With society pressuring us to succeed no matter what the method or moral cost, we must plan how to encounter the temptation to cheat. The following suggestions can provide basic guidelines for making the right decisions and sticking to them.

SET PERSONAL STANDARDS

Determine your personal standards for honesty. Study Bible passages on the topics of honesty, lying, and deceit. From this study, write out your convictions on cheating. Determine beforehand what you will do when you are tempted, regardless of the pressure of circumstances. Make a stand for integrity.

PLAN TO LIVE WITH THE CONSEQUENCES OF YOUR ACTIONS

Most students probably do not study as diligently as they should. Greater self-discipline is a matter of time and growth, but for now the important thing is to decide to live with the consequences of your actions. If you do not study, plan to fail. If you leave homework undone until the last minute, prepare what you can and do not resort to plagiarism. Remember, "Whatever a man sows, this he will also reap" (Galatians 6:7). Do not be tempted to cheat because you lack diligence or discipline. Live with the natural results of your actions.

DEVELOP DISCIPLINE

Everyone experiences some discipline sooner or later in his life. It may be self-discipline, or discipline imposed from an outside source. A self-disciplined person has no need to cheat because he is in control of himself and can recognize the danger of temptation.

Self-discipline allows desires and goals to become realities, and is a basic characteristic of a disciple. The very essence of learning involves discipline of mind and body. Discipline is the key characteristic that will allow you to keep the standards you have set.

DO NOT ALLOW YOUR PEER GROUP TO CONTROL YOU

Peer pressure causes us to do many things we would not normally choose to do. We say and do things that we really do not mean or want to do. The influence of friends and fellow students seems to pressure us beyond our ability to resist.

When this happens, you may find it best to leave your peer group. It is often better to stay and influence them, but at times this is not the wisest choice. Paul said, "Do not be deceived: 'Bad company corrupts good morals'" (1 Corinthians 15:33). Sometimes it is best to run from a pressured situation, and thus control your own actions. When others make your decisions, they control you.

COUNT THE COST

Whenever you are tempted to cheat, take a few minutes and write down the cost. What will be gained—a better grade (maybe), a few hours' sleep, a higher class standing? Then write what you lose—your integrity, a good conscience, a good reputation. When you cheat you are really cheating yourself. You are hurt more than anyone else. You damage your own self-respect and peace of mind. Is it worth the cost?

A few minutes of consideration and praying about this

may save you months and years of grief and remorse. Thomas Jefferson said, "Whenever you do a thing, though it can never be known but to yourself, ask yourself how you would act were all the world looking at you, and act accordingly."

What If You Have Cheated?

Perhaps you have cheated and are convicted about that sin. You are concerned about what course of action you must take now. You cannot change history, so you must live with the results of the past.

As I traveled in India I met one young man who had recently taken his final exams. India generally follows the British system of university education, so his exams covered his entire coursework and determined if he would be granted his degree. He passed, but he cheated. Cheating was common for the exams since they were so important. This student was a Christian, however, and his conscience began to trouble him. Finally, he went to the school authorities and told them he had cheated and therefore would not accept the degree. What would you have done? Would you bear the cost of your actions, or would you rather live with a bad conscience?

Each person must seek God's will in his particular circumstances, but here are a few ideas on how to proceed:

1. *Evaluate the situation objectively.* Memory often grows foggy with time. Even if an incident has been on your mind, the facts about it may be confused. Write out the facts to the best of your ability, then be honest as to whether you did cheat.
2. *Confess to God.* Your cheating may well have hindered your relationship to God for some time. Simply confess the sin to Him (see 1 John 1:9).
3. *Make restitution where possible.* Though this may seem difficult, you must live up to your responsibilities. You may need to contact a teacher or pro-

fessor, or even the administrators of the school. See them personally if you can, or else write. Be simple, factual, and straightforward. Let them know you are a Christian and that this is your reason for correcting the situation.

In several cases I personally have known of, the response to this approach was positive, and no punishment was given. In a few instances, the student received significant punitive action.

If you cheated before becoming a believer, you may need to alter the approach slightly. The incidents may be so numerous that your only choice is to contact an overall administrator. This may be hard, but what price can be attached to a clear conscience?

4. *Decide on new standards*. You must resolve to forego all future cheating. This may take much effort if cheating has been a long-standing habit. Ask God to help you exercise the necessary self-discipline.

Honor, integrity, self-respect—and certainly a clear conscience before God—all are at stake. In the final analysis, when you cheat, you lose.

Notes
1. "An End to Expulsions?" *Newsweek*, 28 March 1977, p. 72.
2. Excerpts from the West Point study are as quoted by Josiah Bunting III, "West Point Counterpoint," *Esquire*, November 1976, p. 130.
3. *Good News* (Fairfield, N.J.: The Economics Press), vol. C, no. 1.
4. Charles F. Kettering, as quoted in *Companion*, September 1977, p. 4.
5. Ilka Chase, as quoted in *The International Encyclopedia of Quotations*, p. 276.
6. Kettering, *Companion*, September 1977, p. 4.

Chapter Nine

HONESTY IN THE CHURCH

———————◦∿◦———————

As the pastor began his sermon the entire church seemed charged with tension. He was nervous, but he spoke with conviction and force. He was carefully weighing every phrase because he knew rumors had raced through the congregation about the events and conflicts of the last week. He wanted to speak specifically to the issues involved, but the feelings were so aroused he stayed with the announced text, though it carried overtones that could be misinterpreted.

He turned slowly to Matthew 5:9, and read carefully, "Blessed are the peacemakers. . . ."

Ray Johnson sat in his regular pew, eyes fixed in a blank stare toward the front of the auditorium. He thought again of the events of Wednesday's board meeting. He had sat tight-lipped as they discussed a decision to procure new blackboards for the classrooms. He abstained in the vote—as he had for the last eight weeks in every financial decision. His stomach knotted as he thought about it again.

The pastor went on, ". . . for they shall be called sons of God."

The blackboards were a small item, really, but the situation had developed into a major issue between him, the pastor, and two others on the board. The discussion on the blackboards had proceeded normally until Ray expressed something that had been bothering him for several months: "I don't think we should spend any more money until we have built up an emergency reserve in the church savings account!"

An antagonistic discussion ensued, centering around faith and finances. The board finally voted for the expenditure—with Ray's abstention. He felt betrayed and unheard. The pastor tried to talk with him, but Ray insisted there was no problem.

Then during the past few days he had told several people that he thought the board and staff were financially irresponsible and that God would not bless the church. Word spread quickly, and he soon regretted his statement. He knew his accusations were dishonest, but his pride would not allow him to make it right. He also knew he had lied when he told the pastor there was no problem.

The pastor went on, "Jesus was the Master Peacemaker. He made the ultimate sacrifice to make peace for us. Are we willing to sacrifice . . . ?"

Willing. Marilyn Green's face flushed with anger. That was the same word the pastor had used yesterday when she was in his office. Against her best judgment she had agreed to meet with the pastor and Betty Arnold. For six months there had been bad feelings—and a few bad words—between Marilyn and Betty, and now their disagreement affected the good relationship their husbands had had for years. The whole church knew about it. Finally the pastor told each of them that they must have a confrontation and reach a resolution. But the meeting was a disaster; neither would admit any wrong.

"The basic requisite for being a peacemaker," the pastor continued, "is that you are personally at peace with God. Many people. . . ."

Jack Barnes moved restlessly in his pew. His conscience stabbed him again. He wondered if the pastor knew. Teaching his Sunday school class became more difficult every week, and attending board meetings depressed him even more. For the past six months he knew he was living in sin. He had covered up several shady actions in his business. His marriage had drifted far from the biblical standard, and he suspected his wife had talked to the pastor as well as others about the problems. Scripturally he knew he was disqualified for church leadership. But he couldn't stand the embarrassment of resigning from his teaching position and the board. Maybe he could stick it out and get his life back in order. . . .

And so it goes. Conflict, misrepresentations, gossip, and false pride chip away at the church. Congregations split. Friendships collapse. Effectiveness sinks. The church's testimony in the community suffers. And it all happens because we have not learned to apply basic principles of honesty in the body of Christ.

HONESTY IN RELATIONSHIPS

The church is people, not programs—and not people in isolation, but people closely relating to one another. The function of a church body consists of these relationships. The lack of them splits churches, fractures friendships, and destroys the church's Christian witness in the community. Most church problems result from breakdowns in personal and spiritual relationships, and frequently the breakdowns happen because of dishonesty.

The need for ethical and truthful standards in these relationships must be emphasized. In spite of many helpful seminars and sermons on body life, fellowship, and church growth, we still fail to preserve the very lifeblood of the church—its members relating in a biblical, honest way.

Principles of Communication

Relationships fail without communication. One gauge of significant communication is the frequent sharing of deeper feelings and thoughts. A dwindling relationship is characterized by such statements as, "We hardly ever talk any more," or "We simply do not share the way we used to." Deep relationships demand communication—effective, honest, and supportive communication.

The various levels of communication have been expressed in these five categories:[1]

> Level 5—*Cliché.* "Hi, how's it going?" "How are you feeling today?" "Great weather, isn't it?" This level does not constitute significant communication, but offers a starting point to higher levels.

> Level 4—*Facts.* "I painted the fence this weekend." "The coal strike ended yesterday." "The boss thinks our production is low." "Marcia told me that food prices went up one percent again last month."

> Level 3—*Ideas.* "I think we would be better off with smaller cars." "My plan for next week is. . . ." "I think the best way to discipline preschoolers is. . . ."

> Level 2—*Feelings.* "I became angry when John told me his plans without even asking what mine were." "I've been discouraged with how my work has been going." "What happened to Ray was really unjust and wrong."

> Level 1—*Total.* This level includes all the other levels and depends on intuitive understanding and

empathy as well as words. No relationship can maintain total communication all of the time. The other levels of communication are needed.

Higher levels of communication involve both effort and risk. But we must venture ahead if relationships are to develop. In the church, especially, our contact with others is often so brief that we must make an additional effort.

We also desperately need credibility as we communicate—credibility that is built on honesty. The old adage, "Say what you mean and mean what you say" reflects good, biblical advice. Paul wrote, "Laying aside falsehood, speak truth, each one of you, with his neighbor, for we are members of one another" (Ephesians 4:25).

On any Sunday in any church, trivial words and questionable communications could fill a book. We say what sounds right or what people expect rather than what we mean, what we think, or what is needed. "Pastor, that was a wonderful message." Was it wonderful? "Hi, Jack, how's work going?" Do we really care?

Honesty does not mean brutality and bluntness. To say you really do not like Mrs. Johnson's hairdo or that the soloist in the service sounded like a howling dog is not edifying. Nor is honesty the necessity to share your deepest self with everyone who asks how you are. Rather, it is saying things that are meaningful, edifying, and truthful.

Consider the following suggestions on how to develop honest and edifying communication in our relationships.

- *Ask God to give you the right motive*—a genuine interest in others. The motive for our communication should be to edify and build up others, rather than to draw attention to ourselves. "There are two types of people in the world: those who come into a room and say, 'Here I am!' and those who come in and say, 'Ah, there you are!'"[2] Paul said, "Do not merely look out for your own personal interests, but also for the interests of others" (Philippians 2:4).

■ *Listen to others*. People desperately want to be heard and listened to. Listening is the foundation for any growing relationship. Learn to listen. Remember names.

■ *Avoid excessive joking and cutting remarks*. Humor has its place, but can easily be misused. Most people become uncomfortable around a person who jokes constantly—especially if they themselves do not like to communicate in that style. Many jokes are camouflaged putdowns, and even the mildest putdowns can hurt people deeply. Humorous communication should never be at the expense of any person.

■ *Learn to ask meaningful questions*. Be alert to what is happening in others' lives. Try to sense what interests them and how they think, and then learn to ask questions about their interests.

■ *Express your views in an honest but non-threatening way*. We want to express what we honestly think, but often we say it in such a way that any contrary opinion would constitute a personal attack on us. We can learn to state our opinion in an honest but inoffensive way. One person says, "I disagree. This church can't allow nonChristians to teach, no matter what the subject." Another would say, "I understand what you mean. However, I do have some reservations on a nonChristian teaching in the church. What was the thought behind your suggestion?"

■ *Do not allow disagreement to break communication*. When you do not agree with someone, make a special effort to speak with them on other topics, and thus enlarge your communication. The "silent treatment" never heals a relationship or increases understanding.

SPECIAL RELATIONSHIPS IN THE CHURCH

The church structure places peculiar demands on certain relationships. Most pastors would need to be omniscient and omnipotent to meet most church members' expectations of them. And church leaders, such as elders, deacons, and teachers, face relationship demands from both the church staff and the congregation.

Pastors are no different from the rest of us in their need and desire for deep personal relationships with special friends. They have limitations on the number of strong relationships they can maintain, yet they are forced into a multitude of situations that require close relationships and communication at every level. Many of these situations are crises, often at the explosion point.

Therefore, honesty in the church demands honesty with the pastor.

The following suggestions can help in our relationships with the pastoral staff.[3]

1. Understand that the pastor and his wife have a private life. They have needs for special friendships that do not relate directly to the functioning of the church. Many pastors are criticized if they become too "thick" with another couple. Jealousy builds and gossip and criticism prevail. Although Christians should be able to relate to any other Christian, we know there are certain people with whom we "click" and naturally form a healthy relationship. So be honest. Give the pastor the same privilege you give yourself.
2. Take the initiative in your relationships with the

staff. Do not wait for them to make the first move and then criticize them when they do not. But be careful not to monopolize them in public situations. Help them meet new people.

3. Do not put unrealistic demands and expectations on the pastor's wife. The church hired him, not his wife. Certainly she needs to be supportive of his ministry but her prime objective is to be a godly woman, wife, and mother.

4. Remember that every pastor has weaknesses and limitations. One man will relate beautifully to people, but not preach or teach well. Another will shine in the pulpit, but not foster warm relationships. Another may plan and organize well but lack ability in other areas. We must have honest and realistic expectations of those we select to lead us spiritually.

5. Criticize and make suggestions in private. Frequently, the pastor is the last one to hear that a particular person disagrees with him about something. Biblical honesty requires that we share our concerns or criticisms directly with the person responsible for what we dislike. Present your concern as soon as you have carefully thought about it—before bitterness or a bad attitude builds. Share your concern in kindness, with a willingness to listen and learn. The pastor may be totally unaware of the problem or offense, and simply need information to make a correction.

6. Encourage and compliment him. A note like this is an example:

Dear Pastor,

Your message Sunday was excellent. I appreciated the emphasis you made on personally applying the teaching to my life. Keep

up the good work. I pray for you daily.
Thanks.

The little extra effort to write that note is better than a hundred "Good message, Pastor" greetings at the church door. He needs personal encouragement that he is doing a good job. He will certainly hear about the negatives anyway. Be an honest encourager. If you are, when you later have a constructive criticism the pastor will give you a listening and receptive ear.

7. Give the pastor positive and honest support. When others begin to criticize him, defend him honestly and encourage the other person to talk to the pastor rather than continuing to talk to others. Backbiting and gossip destroy the spiritual fiber of the church. They are dishonest and unbiblical.

Let us examine also the relationships of other church leaders to the pastor and people. Leaders in the church—elders, deacons, teachers—must relate to the church staff, the congregation, and to each other. Each of these relationships has a certain set of demands. These people normally meet frequently as a small group or with the church staff. Although this presents good opportunities to develop relationships, these meetings usually contain mostly business with little personal interaction in other areas.

In any type of corporate leadership there will be disagreements. Without close personal relationships, these differences can lead to division and problems. When mutual trust and friendship exist, differences become a time of learning and maturing as the group seeks God's will together.

The following suggestions for church leaders are not comprehensive in this area, but stress some of the key issues a leader faces in his relationships.

1. *Honest relationships are a major part of your responsibility*. A leader cannot lead unless he relates to people. Titles and position are meaningless if the leader isolates himself from honest interaction with persons at all levels of the church. Take the matter of relationships seriously.

2. *Develop an honest friendship with the pastor and staff*. Friendship bridges many gaps of opinion and philosophy. "Above all, keep fervent in your love for one another, because love covers a multitude of sins" (1 Peter 4:8). Friendship is based on love. Learn and understand the pastor's heart, his way of thinking, and his plans.

3. *Honestly and positively support the decisions of the church leadership*. Support for decisions isn't a problem when you fully agree with them. But what happens when you are opposed to them? Do you sulk and sow seeds of discontent, hopefully waiting for the plan to collapse? If so, you deny that a group of godly people can corporately find God's will. That is the purpose of team decisions — to guard against a one-man show (yours or someone else's). To be honest before God you must believe that the direction was right, and support it wholeheartedly as though it were your own. Be willing to let God lead the team, and even to change your thinking.

4. *Learn to express your view honestly in a non-threatening manner*. We all experience difficulty in discussing issues about which we feel strongly—whether these feelings are influenced by conviction, prejudice, or background. If we maintain honest relationships as a group of leaders, we will be able to express our views and know that others will listen and understand. We will also permit others to reject our ideas and to teach us different ways of thinking and operating.

Avoid speaking in frustration or anger. Such emotions place others at a disadvantage, and lead to disagreements rather than godly discussion. Be a student of yourself. Learn how to express your views in a way that persuades rather than aggravates. "You cannot antagonize and persuade at the same time."[4]

5. Avoid group confrontations. It is intimidating and humiliating to be confronted in a group. Whenever possible, discuss things in private before issues come to a board or planning group. A good leader will share his ideas and plans privately with several members of the group before bringing them up for public discussion. A person who is embarrassed or put down before a group can be deeply hurt. Months may be needed to rebuild the rapport. "A brother offended is harder to be won than a strong city" (Proverbs 18:19).

6. *Be an honest and accurate filter for the pastor and staff*. Some of the best feedback and information for the pastoral staff can come through the church leaders. People will talk to leaders when they will not talk with the pastor. Know what the congregation is thinking and feeling about the affairs of the church, and accurately communicate their ideas to other leaders and the staff.

7. *Keep lines of communication open with the people in the congregation*. We can easily isolate ourselves within a small circle of friends. But leaders are responsible to relate more broadly than we may personally desire to do. We must learn to ask questions and probe for the sense and direction of the people.

REQUIREMENTS FOR RELATING

After a series of difficult encounters with people and a few rebuffs of friendship, most of us begin thinking, "I just can't seem to develop good relationships, no matter how hard I try." But we can learn certain basic characteristics that undergird relating well to people. Consider these characteristics for your own life.

1. *Be a teachable person*. The greatest block to growth in personal relationships is an unteachable spirit. Everyone has something to share and wants to be heard and believed.

Everyone also knows *something* that you do not.

An unteachable person presents a great hindrance to the growth and development of the church. When a person stops learning, he begins to die mentally and emotionally. "The way of a fool is right in his own eyes, but a wise man is he who listens to counsel" (Proverbs 12:15).

Why are we reluctant to learn from others? Pride. We simply do not want to admit our needs or our lack of knowledge. The learner is always placed in an inferior position. Jesus said, "A pupil is not above his teacher" (Luke 6:40). But we resist that posture.

A key issue of discipleship (in fact, the very meaning of the word) is teachability. The disciple of Jesus Christ will be a learner and will consequently win people's hearts as he learns from them.

We will never know the joy of relationships until we let others become our teachers. People respond when they are on their "own turf." Learn to fish from a man who knows how to fish. Learn to make bread in that special way from the woman who knows. Ask your neighbor to teach you to tune your automobile engine. Ask them what they do at work. You will be amazed at how relationships begin to develop. Be a learner. Be a person who opens his mind to others and lets them know he is willing to learn.

2. *Do not be an opinionated person.* Have you met the person who has a definite, unmovable opinion on everything? Taxes—he knows the perfect solution. Doctrine—he clicks off his pet beliefs like a machine. Children—he's an expert, having raised two of them. Change—he's against it. Politics—by now you wish you hadn't asked.

So you have met him too? We all have. And no one really likes him. An opinionated person has few friends. He doesn't communicate because he doesn't discuss. Relating to an opinionated person is like relating to a book—once printed, it never changes.

Lest we sound too righteous, we need to admit that we all are a bit like this. We all have "blind spots." We can look back on times when we fervently expressed our opinion and lost a listening friend.

Recently I was on a long trip with a close friend and associate. We began talking about education—schools, discipline, accreditation standards, and philosophy of teaching. I expounded my opinions on a particular issue with all the force of a football runner's stiff arm.

Later I reflected on the fact that my friend had a master's degree and almost a doctorate in education, and had been a teacher, vice principal, and principal in elementary, junior high, and high school. Although I had taught at the university level, I had never had an education course, never taught in a public school, and certainly had never evaluated a school or program or curriculum in any real way. As I thought on our conversation, I felt a bit embarrassed—in fact, stupid. He listened politely to my "wisdom" and graciously said very little—but how could he? I had closed the door on any discussion. Realizing what I had done, I later apologized to him.

We need to be honest in our opinions and ideas, but tactful in how we express them. If we come across as opinionated and obstinate, we close the door to many valuable relationships. True convictions do not need door-slamming emotions to support them. We must share with the openness of a learner, and the honesty of one who has spent time prayerfully reflecting on the issues at hand.

3. *Hear the other person's viewpoint.* Listening is not hearing. Hearing involves comprehension and understanding—not just a tape-recorded reply of what was said. In my family I have the reputation of listening and doing something else at the same time. I can repeat exactly what was said, yet I did not truly hear. On occasion, to get my *real* attention, one of the family says, "Today I went to the library and got a book on horses. I need to do a report for English. . . . Then after

that I plan to go outside, eat some sand, and commit suicide!" They usually hope I won't hear the sarcastic switch to nonsense. I do, but they are right. I was not truly hearing.

Hearing involves serious consideration of what is being said. Communication and relationships are quickly disrupted by one who interrupts another to argue his viewpoint. Listen, hear, and understand before speaking. In this way we can come to know much more about another person, and knowing the person is a mandatory part of developing a relationship. And who knows? If you listen to others, they might even listen to you.

4. *Be a servant.* Unpaid, volunteer servants are rare. We are conditioned to serve only when we expect something in return—service to us, or recognition. But Jesus said, "The Son of Man did not come to be served, but to serve, and to give His life a ransom for many" (Matthew 20:28). And He tells us, "Do good, and lend, expecting nothing in return" (Luke 6:35).

As we begin to develop relationships, we must learn to serve without expecting others to reciprocate our dinner invitations or pay back our favors. True giving and serving is directed to those who cannot repay us. To build relationships, look for ways you can help others.

HONESTY IN CONFLICT

Conflict is the norm in growth and life in the church, yet we try to avoid it at all costs. Something inside us says that conflict is wrong and unhealthy. Conflict drains us emotionally and disturbs the tranquility of our concept of close relationships. But conflict handled biblically and honestly causes growth and maturing that can come in no other way.

If a church is to survive, succeed, and grow, the congregation and its leaders must learn to cope with conflict.

But most churches collapse instead of cope. Conflict begins in a small unobtrusive way, festering in the minds of a few but hidden from others. Then it slowly emerges, and finally explodes and divides. People become angry and leave the church. Meanwhile the next conflict is brewing and the process repeats itself. But this process is unbiblical, dishonest, and unnecessary.

Conflict and its resolution can demonstrate the solidarity of relationships in the church. The following simple rules can significantly affect the outcome of conflict in the church, making it healthy instead of harmful.

1. *Identify the conflict to yourself as soon as possible.* Frequently we refuse to admit that conflict is present. Early identification will help you deal with it before it intensifies uncontrollably.

2. *Express the conflict to a neutral person,* preferably someone who can have a part in resolving the conflict.

3. *Surface the conflict as early as possible in open discussion.* This is always your responsibility. If you have a problem with someone, you are responsible scripturally to make the first move (Matthew 18:15). If you know someone has a problem with you, you also are bound to make the first move (5:23-24). It is always your duty.

4. *Be willing to compromise or admit you are wrong.* Most conflict in churches comes not over significant doctrinal issues, but over preferences, relationships, and minor incidents. A willingness to "give in" and swallow your pride will aid immeasurably in healing conflict.

5. *Be honest, but not brutal.* Express your thoughts and ideas honestly, but without cutting down another person or his ideas. If you do not express

your true thoughts in discussion, the issue will diffuse outwardly, but still fester inwardly.

6. *Allow restitution of relationships.* We would be foolish and idealistic to expect everyone to agree on everything. But differing opinions on issues need not be reason for broken relationships and conflict. When a conflict occurs, the first goal is restitution of the relationship. The issue itself may be resolved only slowly or never, but the relationship must continue.

Many people become defensive and tense when any disagreements with their views emerge. They equate agreement with friendship. We need to learn to live with a measure of disagreement and difference of opinion. What a dull world it would be if everyone agreed with us! Someone has said that if two people always agree, one of them is unnecessary.

Honesty forms the basis for relationships in the church. Conflict and its resolution demonstrate the solidarity of those relationships.[5]

HONESTY IN LEADERSHIP

Severe struggles develop when a leader in the church does not meet the scriptural qualifications for a leader. The reputation of any church will waver and crack when people in the community know that the real life of one of its leaders violates their sense of ethics and morality. The reputation of both the local church and Jesus Christ is borne by the church's leaders. Their lives must match their public stand.

Who are the leaders in the church? Anyone who fills a position of responsibility or who purposefully exerts influence on others is a leader. Pastors, elders, deacons, Sunday school teachers, Bible study leaders, administrators, choir directors, and youth leaders are all in this category.

Whose responsibility is it to see that these leaders meet scriptural qualifications for their specific position? Theoretically it is the responsibility of the church body and its leaders. But what if those presently in leadership are not qualified to choose, or they appoint without investigation? Ultimately the responsibility falls on the person being chosen. We must depend on his honesty to determine his own qualifications.

As a current or potential leader, then, you must examine yourself honestly to determine if you qualify. Several issues stand out in this consideration.

HYPOCRISY

"I wouldn't go to that church in a million years! I know some of their leaders and they are a bunch of hypocrites." Sound familiar? These comments are especially prevalent in small communities. We would like to deny these allegations, plead ignorance, or write them off as the antagonistic remarks of nonChristians. But, unfortunately, too often they ring true.

The Scriptures speak directly about hypocrisy. In his letter to the Romans, Paul severely criticized Jews who did not live up to what they taught:

> If you bear the name "Jew," and rely upon the Law, and boast in God, and know His will, and approve the things that are essential, being instructed out of the Law, and are confident that you yourself are a guide to the blind, a light to those who are in darkness, a corrector of the foolish, a teacher of the immature, having in the Law the embodiment of knowledge and of the truth, you, therefore, who teach another, do you not teach yourself? You who preach that one

should not steal, do you steal? You who say that one should not commit adultery, do you commit adultery? You who abhor idols, do you rob temples? You who boast in the Law, through your breaking the Law, do you dishonor God? For "the name of God is blasphemed among the Gentiles because of you," just as it is written. (Romans 2:17-24)

This is the basic definition of hypocrisy—teaching or saying one thing and doing another. And the result is that "the name of God is blasphemed."

No one lives a life before God and men so perfectly that he is blameless. Each of us still needs to grow and develop spiritually. Yet there is a minimum level of maturity needed for those in leadership. It is not uncommon for people to be in leadership positions who do not read the Bible and pray daily, who do not study Scripture for themselves, and who do not obey what they know to do in the Christian life. They are in the position simply out of the congregation's need or by democratic vote. Some have served as Christian leaders when they were not even Christians.

Perhaps your conscience is speaking to you about hypocrisy in your own life. Do not allow yourself to continue in a double-minded lifestyle. If there are problems or sins in your life that are obvious to you, the only honest thing to do is to remove yourself from the leadership position until you have dealt with them. You may be thinking, "But that would be so embarrassing. Why can't I just take care of the problems while I continue in my position?" This is possible if the sin is minor, but usually you cannot reverse your direction so easily. It takes time to change. It takes courage to admit your need.

If you know your life does not match your mouth, do not hesitate to take bold action to make things right. It may be the first real step of maturity you have made. Living a double standard will never bring peace and blessing to your life. Moses warned the Hebrews, "You have sinned against the Lord, and be sure your sin will find you out" (Numbers 32:23). Will you take care of it now or will you wait until God reveals it later?

OPEN SIN

A leader comes under great pressure from Satan to commit sin that disqualifies him. Saul sinned and lost his kingdom (1 Samuel 15). Moses sinned and God prevented him from entering the promised land (Numbers 20:1-13). David sinned and God sent great sorrow into his life (2 Samuel 11–12). A leader in sin puts himself in a precarious position before God. James wrote, "Let not many of you become teachers, my brethren, knowing that as such we shall incur a stricter judgment" (James 3:1).

Specific known sin in a leader's life prevents him from usefulness to God in his position. He may still function, but he cannot be blessed. And the longer he hides the sin, the more dulled his senses become to the leading of God's Spirit.

Leaders must deal ruthlessly with sin. Guard against immorality, dishonesty in your work, and prejudice and hostility in church matters. If you are now in a circumstance of open sin, take action immediately to extract yourself and make restitution. Do not let sin destroy your usefulness to God—as an individual Christian or as a leader.

MATURITY

The need of the hour in church leadership is men and women who are gifted, called by God, and mature. But even the gifted and called can lack true spiritual maturity.

What is maturity? Is it gray hair and Bible knowledge? Is it sage wisdom and common sense? Is it patience and love? Is it dependence on prayer and the leading of God?

Yes—and more. The spiritual maturing process never ends. But it does begin. And some have not begun. A. W. Tozer aptly states our need:

> The church at this moment needs men, the right kind of men, bold men. . . .
>
> We languish for men who feel themselves expendable in the warfare of the soul, who cannot be frightened by threats of death because they have already died to the allurements of this world. Such men will be free from the compulsions that control weaker men. They will not be forced to do things by the squeeze of circumstances; their only compulsion will come from within—or from above.
>
> . . . They will make no decisions out of fear, take no course out of a desire to please, accept no service for financial considerations, perform no religious act out of mere custom, nor will they allow themselves to be influenced by the love of publicity or the desire for reputation.[6]

In Hebrews we read, "For though by this time you ought to be teachers, you have need again for someone to teach you the elementary principles of the oracles of God. . . . But solid food is for the mature, who because of *practice* have their senses trained to discern good and evil" (Hebrews 5:12,14; emphasis added).

We lack mature men and women in the leadership of the church. We lack people who have grown from spiritual infancy into responsible spiritual adulthood. One may have been a Christian for twenty years and still be a babe in the spiritual sense. But because of longevity we thrust him into a position of leadership, and we reap the results.

Identifying maturity in someone else is risky at best. One may be a mature *person*, but not a mature *Christian*.

But there are ways to gauge your own maturity level. No checklist can perfectly define maturity, but perhaps this brief list can help you begin an evaluation of yourself.

- *A mature Christian has an understanding of Scripture.* Knowledge of God's Word is basic to growth and maturity. The Hebrews passage quoted above tells of people who should have known the Word, but did not.
- *A mature Christian applies Scripture to his daily life.* Knowledge without application erodes the very meaning of the Christian life—seeing our lives changed into the image of Christ. The person who regularly allows the Bible to alter his life evidences maturity. Again, the passage in Hebrews speaks of those who "because of practice have their senses trained to discern good and evil." Practice implies action and application. Training implies a process of experience and growth. Practice and training precede maturity.
- *A mature Christian is not a new convert.* Paul warned that a Christian leader should not be a new convert, "lest he become conceited and fall into the condemnation incurred by the devil" (1 Timothy 3:6). A new convert needs to grow spiritually, not lead spiritually.
- *A mature Christian has gone through testing.* Paul also said that leaders should "first be tested; then let them serve as deacons if they are beyond reproach" (1 Timothy 3:10). Personal growth is closely related to our experience in walking with God. We cannot gain instant experience, so time is needed for growth and testing. Testing is not necessarily suffering, but involves being proven in faithfulness in the church and its ministry.

- *A mature Christian clearly demonstrates Christian character.* Love, joy, patience, gentleness, and many other characteristics listed in Galatians 5:22-23 provide evidence of Christian character. Evidences of immaturity are anger, impatience, harsh words, and a critical spirit. Christlike character is the foundation of Christian maturity.
- *A mature Christian is stable and consistent.* A mark of immaturity is impulsive, unstable reactions to adverse situations. Stability develops from a dependent walk with God—knowing that He will lead and provide even in adverse circumstances. Consistency of life also indicates maturity—consistency in our actions, in our personal walk with God, and in seeking answers from His Word.

Again, the burden of decision rests on those being selected for leadership. Do you meet the standard of maturity? If not, what do you lack? What can you do to develop and become mature and qualified? Be honest in your evaluation, and express it to those who want you to lead.

Scriptural Qualifications for Leadership

Scripture carefully outlines the qualifications of a leader in 1 Timothy 3 and Titus 1.[7]

Consider 1 Timothy 3:2-13:

An overseer, then, must be above reproach, the husband of one wife, temperate, prudent, respectable, hospitable, able to teach, not addicted to wine or pugnacious, but gentle, uncontentious, free from the love of money. He must be one who manages his own household well, keeping his children under control with all dignity (but if a man does not know how to manage his own household, how will he take care of the church of God?); and not a new convert, lest he become conceited and fall into the condemnation incurred by the devil. And he must have a good reputation with those outside the church, so that he may not fall into reproach and the snare of the devil. Deacons likewise must be men of dignity, not double-tongued, or addicted to much wine or fond of sordid gain, but holding to the mystery of the faith with a clear conscience. And let these also first be tested; then let them serve as deacons if they are beyond reproach. Women must likewise be dignified, not malicious gossips, but temperate, faithful in all things. Let deacons be husbands of only one wife, and good managers of their children and their own households. For those who have served well as deacons obtain for themselves a high standing and great confidence in the faith that is in Christ Jesus.

Now, let's be honest. Do we really select a potential leader in our church on the basis of these qualifications? Frequently we simply pick the available, the willing, and the faithful.

Let us look particularly at three qualifications from this passage that need emphasis.

1. *He must be uncontentious* (verse 3). We do not need fighters. We desperately need leaders who will lead in a quiet, godly manner without the contentiousness of the world's system. "A gentle answer turns away wrath, but a harsh word stirs up anger. The tongue of the wise makes knowledge acceptable, but the mouth of fools spouts folly" (Proverbs 15:1-2).

2. *He must have a good reputation with those outside the church* (verse 7). A man's reputation at work affects his function in the church. We can learn much about a man's spiritual life by talking with nonChristians who know him. If his reputation in the world is tarnished, he negates the reputation of the church when he becomes a leader. And the result of a bad reputation is that he may "fall into reproach and the snare of the devil." This snare is that we force him to live a hypocritical life, and his guilt eventually destroys him.

3. *He must not be double-tongued* (verse 8). God places a premium on verbal honesty and speech free of gossip. The leader must be a man of wise and dependable speech. He does not have the luxury of idle speech and careless words.

We should note also (verse 11) that this passage lists qualifications for women serving in leadership roles—positions such as deaconesses, teachers, and Bible study leaders.

CALLING

Finally, a leader must be called by God both to leadership and to a particular function. We do not "draft" leaders; rather, we find God's will for a certain person at a particular time. That person must make sure God has called him to a particular task, and then do it with all his heart.

A need does not constitute a call. A few years ago I was asked to lead a choir in a small church. I expressed that I probably would not, but that I would pray about it. After praying, I confirmed that I did not believe God was leading me to direct the choir. The reply was, "But you've got to. There is no one else in the church who can do it." I replied, "Then it is obvious that God is leading us to cancel the choir!" However, someone else did take over the task of directing the choir. God provides all the leadership needed for every vital function of the church.

Do not allow a "draft" or "need" to be your only call. On the other hand, be available wherever God wants to use you as a leader.

HONESTY AND THE CHURCH'S EFFECTIVENESS

In any organization, programs and activities can outlast their need and yet continue for years filling the time and energy of its people. In the church, perhaps the most crucial question is "Are we meeting the true needs of the people?" Tradition and the lack of honest evaluation can keep us locked into forms, schedules, concepts, and activities that long ago ceased to meet true needs. Therefore, we need to honestly evaluate the structure and programs of our church.

To honestly meet needs in the church, several things must be done.

Evaluate needs. You cannot meet needs about which you know nothing. Talk with people. Take surveys. Ask for honest ideas about the effectiveness of every activity in your church—from the worship service to the nursery to every committee. Be totally honest. For even greater objectivity, have someone outside the church help you evaluate.

Evaluate the programs. Once the needs are determined, examine each program in the church to determine if it helps people in their spiritual lives and if it is meeting specific needs. If a program exists that meets no visible need, be honest enough to eliminate it.

Develop true fellowship. One of the most vital functions of the church is fellowship—not the fellowship of church dinners and social events, but of people openly sharing their lives with each other. This is not feeling-oriented sharing, or "here's everything I think and feel" type of interaction, but rather the fellowship based on honest relationships where people share real needs—and are heard and helped. The church must develop and spawn this special kind of fellowship. The best teaching and most stimulating activities will fall on deaf ears without the life-giving sharing of biblical fellowship.

Help your church grow by outreach. One of the church's main functions is to reach out to the world. Are we seeing people enter our midst through conversion rather than adoption from other churches and transfers? Without evangelistic outreach by individuals and groups, the church will soon turn inward and die.

Honesty in our churches will promote genuine fellowship, capable leadership, and effective outreach. Such honesty will be blessed by God, and will enhance the experiences of the church inwardly and outwardly.

Notes
1. John Powell, *Why Am I Afraid to Tell You Who I Am?* (Niles, Ill.: Argus Communications, 1969), pp. 54-64.
2. *Bits and Pieces*, November 1973, p. 9.
3. More ideas can be found in the book by Wes Roberts, *Support Your Local Pastor* (Colorado Springs, Colo.: NavPress, 1995).
4. *Bits and Pieces*, April 1975.
5. A good reference for handling conflict is *Caring Enough to Confront* by David Augsburger (Glendale, Calif.: Regal Books, 1973).
6. A. W. Tozer, *Of God and Men* (Harrisburg, Penn.: Christian Publications, 1960), pp. 14-15.
7. Gene A. Getz discusses these scriptural qualifications for church leaders in *The Measure of a Man* (Glendale, Calif.: Regal Books, 1974).

Chapter Ten

HONESTY WITH YOURSELF

―――――――――――⌒∽――――――――――

The following letter was received by the president of a Christian youth organization, from a recipient of some of the organization's awards. Certain specifics have been altered to protect the writer's identity.

Dear Sirs:

Enclosed you will find awards that I am returning to you. Let me explain. They were obtained dishonestly. When I moved from one city to another, I was behind everyone else in the program so I forged the initials of my former leader to a number of requirements. It was enough to put me well on my way toward [the highest award]. All these years my life has been a lie. The Lord has recently touched me in a new and wonderful way, and I praise God for the convicting power of the Holy Spirit. . . . I even served a church as a pastor for seven months. All of which I am deeply ashamed about because I was not able to be used of God because of this unconfessed sin in my life.

Presently, I am wanting to again serve a church as a pastor . . . but I need to "clean up my act" so I can be used fully by Him. . . . I have no right to teach others about Christ and not live what I teach. I always knew that, but never applied it. . . .

I hope and pray that you can forgive me. I know God has, and God now can use me in His service . . . .

I feel through this experience I have learned many valuable lessons that can help other young men to avoid making the same mistakes I have made. . . .

I know it is difficult for you to picture a "cheater" as a leader and I would pray that the Lord would give you a forgiving spirit.

Years of inner turmoil for this person were finally resolved. And his first step was total honesty with himself.

How honest are you with yourself? Do you live in a dream world—or even a nightmare? When you view yourself, what do you see? How honestly we view ourselves in every area of life will greatly affect how honestly we view God and other people.

SELF-DECEPTION

Though we may not consciously deceive others, we become masters at deceiving ourselves. We argue with ourselves, lie to ourselves, refuse to believe truth about ourselves, and generally shield ourselves from anything that would disturb and disrupt our private world.

Whatever we do, we must be convinced that our actions are justified. We cannot live for long with a conflict between our actions and our knowledge of right. So when we do wrong, we often use self-deception to convince ourselves that our actions were right.

To do this we embark on a long process of rationalization, frequently in the form of a series of self-deceiving thoughts:

It probably wasn't the best thing to do, but I really had no choice.

I know the Bible seems to say this is wrong, but I'm sure there are several interpretations of those passages.

I talked to the pastor and he didn't tell me it was wrong. I know I didn't tell him all the circumstances but he knew enough to help me.

What's done is done. I can't reverse it so I had better live with it.

If I change now, people will know I was wrong before.

I have seen other Christians do the same thing—so it must be okay.

And finally,

I'm convinced that I am right in what I did.

If we use Scripture at all in this process, we are tempted to reinterpret passages that tend to make us uncomfortable. We all have the strong urge to justify our actions, no matter what the cost. And the cost is self-deception.

The Scriptures address the problem of self-deception directly. "Be ye doers of the word and not hearers only, *deceiving your own selves*" (James 1:22, KJV, emphasis added). A person who only hears the Word and does not obey it deceives himself. We can hear Scripture, and even agree with it, but if the agreeing does not result in personal obedience, the process of self-deception has begun. James also said, "Anyone who listens to the Word but does not do what it says is like a man who looks at his face in a mirror and, after looking at himself, goes away and immediately forgets what he looks like" (1:23-24, NIV). Self-deceit begins with the refusal to face truth. A mirror accurately reflects a person's face, but he may refuse to remember what he sees.

Paul wrote, "Do not deceive yourselves. If any one of you

thinks he is wise by the standards of this age, he should become a 'fool' so that he may become wise" (1 Corinthians 3:18, NIV). To think you are wise without understanding God's Word and His standards is self-deception.

Self-deception can take the form of either justifying sin or not believing God can use you. The whole process occurs so subtly that we hardly notice it is happening. Guarding against it takes effort and faith, because our minds and emotions rebel against truth. The following suggestions may help you avoid self-deception.

- *Be blunt with yourself.* When your mind is struggling with an issue, write down the facts to see the situation objectively.
- *Be honest with God's Word.* Do not rationalize Scripture to fit your need. Above all, find out what the Bible says.
- *When you sin, admit it.* Do not justify sin. Be direct and forthright with God. Confess any known sin.
- *Respond to the urgings of your conscience.* In areas where the Bible is not specific, you must rely on the general teaching of the Word and your conscience.
- *Keep a focus on truth.* Do not avoid the truth. It may hurt, but in the long run it will heal. You have nothing to fear from the truth—either in the form of facts or Scripture.

An old prayer says,

> From the cowardice that shrinks from new truths,
> From the laziness that is content with half-truths,
> From the arrogance that thinks it knows all truth,
> O God of Truth, deliver us.[1]

We must face up to the facts. "A man who will not admit he has been wrong loves himself more than he loves the truth."[2] Self-deceit must be countered with a deliberate and conscious grasp for honesty. There is no bliss in ignorance. We must press for truth with ourselves.

HONESTY WITH GOD

God has a clear purpose for each of us and wants us to follow His plan for us. Yet we become so intent on our own goals and plans that we do not respond to God in an honest way. Without honestly relating to God, we may experience problems of legalism or a wrong self-image.

LEGALISM AND SELF-IMPOSED ETHICS

Many Christians are paralyzed in their spiritual lives because they do not understand that we cannot work our way to salvation. Paul said, "By grace you have been saved through faith; and that not of yourselves, it is the gift of God; not as a result of works, that no one should boast" (Ephesians 2:8-9). God is a God of grace. Salvation is His free gift. We can never earn it. Yet we still attempt to live the Christian life as though our salvation depended totally on our actions. We put ourselves under a burden of legalism. Intellectually we may understand the doctrine of grace, but practically we govern our lives by law.

We are not honest with God when we set up rules for ourselves and expect to maintain our relationship with Him by keeping them. We do need standards for living, but we must not confuse these standards with salvation and our relationship to God. We deceive ourselves when we think that obeying a set of rules or a self-imposed set of ethical standards is the substance of our standing with God. Rules and the ethical standards can be right and good, but they cannot establish or replace our getting to know God personally.

When we understand where ethical decisions fit in God's plan — that they are to result from our fellowship with God, rather than determine our standing with Him — our minds and hearts can be greatly freed from pressure. We can then obey and respond to God on the basis of love rather than fear.[3]

As you develop personal convictions and make ethical decisions, guard against legalism. If you set standards and rules for yourself, do so out of love for God, not out of law.

SELF-IMAGE

To be honest with yourself and God you must have a biblical and sane view of yourself. Many recent books have been written that approach the topics of self-realization, self-actualization, and self-image from many sides, but certain truths need to be reemphasized here.

The first step of honesty in self-image is to see yourself as God sees you. You may shudder at that idea, knowing the inner thoughts of your heart and your past actions. But remember that God sees you in love through the cross of Jesus Christ. He sees you as forgiven. Since you received Jesus Christ as Savior, God now sees and treats you as a beloved son or daughter, not as an enemy. Paul said, "In Him we have redemption through His blood, the forgiveness of our trespasses, according to the riches of His grace, which He lavished upon us" (Ephesians 1:7-8). Yet, God still sees your needs and problems, and He works to train and develop you as His child.

God sees each of us as a unique person of great value to Him. He cares for us personally, and not just as a statistic or another face. He treats us individually according to our growth, maturity, and needs. He made us just like we are. We must accept ourselves as we are.

As I was growing up I imagined myself as having buck-teeth and large ears. In college when one person referred to me as "Handles" because of my ears, I cringed. I looked down on myself. As I matured in Christ, I realized that my appearance did not matter to God and that I could be thankful for it. I had to be honest with myself as to how I appeared to others. As a matter of fact, I did not have protruding teeth and my ears were not all that large. But in all honesty I had to admit that I was not an imposing person in appearance or personality. God simply had to use me as I was, not as I hoped to be.

Whether you are tall, short, slender, or fat; whether you have a big nose, freckles, a pretty smile, or a good build, God loves you and made you just as you are. In fact, He made you as you are to use you in a special way. Beauty and handsomeness are surface qualities that diminish as the body ages. Security is never found in appearance, but only in a satisfying relationship with God.

Self-image is basically self-acceptance. To accept yourself as you are, acknowledging that God made you that way, is the epitome of self-honesty. Paul said, "Be honest in your estimate of yourselves, measuring your value by how much faith God has given you" (Romans 12:3, TLB). Most of us vacillate between a feeling of absolute worthlessness in some areas to an inflated ego in others. Rarely do we see ourselves objectively. But we must strive to do so.

For some the problem is egotism. "If anyone thinks he is something when he is nothing," Paul said, "he deceives himself" (Galatians 6:3). Paul also referred to selfish conceit as being empty—conceit when there is nothing to be conceited about (Philippians 2:3).

The problem for others is that they think they are worthless. Jesus said, "Are not five sparrows sold for two cents? And yet not one of them is forgotten before God. Indeed, the very hairs of your head are all numbered. Do not fear; you are of more value than many sparrows" (Luke 12:6-7). God said to Israel, "I have loved you with an everlasting love" (Jeremiah 31:3). You are valuable in God's sight.

Not only does God love you deeply, but He will also

greatly use your life. For many who have little outward ability it may seem that God cannot use you even a little, much less greatly. But you may not realize how fully God has used you already, or plans to in the future.

Several years ago a professor at Johns Hopkins University assigned a group of graduate students to go to the slums and investigate the backgrounds and environments of 200 boys between the ages of twelve and sixteen, and then predict their chances for success in the future. After researching social statistics, talking to the boys, and gathering as much data as they could, the students concluded that 90 percent of the boys would spend time in jail.

Twenty-five years later another group of graduate students was given the job of going back to the same slum area and testing that prediction. Some of the boys—now men—were still there; a few had died and some had moved away. But the students were able to contact 180 of the original 200, and they found that only four of the group had ever been sent to jail.

Why did these men, who had grown up in a breeding place of crime, have such a surprisingly good record? The researchers were continually told, "Well, there was this teacher. . . ."

They searched further and found that 75 percent of the boys had been influenced by a particular woman. The researchers found her living in a home for retired teachers, and asked her how she had exerted such a remarkable influence over a group of slum children. Could she give them any reason why these boys should have remembered her?

"No," she said, "no, I really couldn't." And then, thinking back over the years, she said more to herself than to her questioners, "I loved those boys. . . ."[4]

Can you honestly say you believe God can and will use you? God can, and He will.

SELF-EVALUATION

Realistically, we must recognize that we possess both limitations and gifts. We need to look objectively in the mirror of experience and counsel to see our weaknesses as well as our strengths. Self-evaluation is difficult and elusive, but it can help you be honest about your strengths, abilities, weaknesses, and gifts. As a start, a few suggestions for honestly evaluating yourself are listed below.

1. *Pray.* Pray for clarity of thought and objectivity as you begin the process.
2. *Set aside time.* You need two or three hours to think and pray through your evaluation. Do not try to do it in a few minutes.
3. *Be thinking about it ahead of time.* A few days before your evaluation, think about your strengths and needs. Jot them down as they come to mind.
4. *Make a list.* As you begin your time, divide your paper into the categories of strengths and abilities on one hand, and weaknesses and needs on the other. Strengths and abilities are the things you naturally lean toward or do well—for example, organizing projects, helping others, making mechanical repairs, or motivating people. Weaknesses and needs are things you cannot do well, and areas in which you can make specific improvement—humility, controlling your tongue, organizing your time. Simply jot down whatever comes to mind—regardless of how minor it may seem.
5. *Write down things you enjoy.* List some things you enjoy doing whether they are part of your job or leisure activities. This will give you a clue as to your gifts and strengths.
6. *Ask others for their evaluation.* Others, especially

your spouse, can help in giving you insight into yourself. Take notes as they share with you.

7. *Take a formal evaluation.* I recommend taking the Taylor-Johnson Temperament Analysis Test. Many pastors and counselors are trained in administering this test. It is simple and brief, and will give you insight into your own personality. Two other personal evaluation options are the Meyers-Briggs Type Indicator and the DISC test. Several books on temperament and personality are readily available.[5]

8. *Draw some conclusions.* Sift through your notes and evaluations and write out specific conclusions in the areas of strengths and weaknesses, natural abilities, spiritual gifts, current needs, and personality. This process will give you a good start on understanding yourself. From your conclusions, set priorities and personal objectives for changes you want to make in your life.

In his book *Roots* Alex Haley describes the birth of his ancestor in Africa in this way: "Omoro then walked to his wife's side, leaned over the infant and, as all watched, whispered into his son's ear the name he had chosen for him. Omoro's people felt that each human being should be the first to know who he was."[6]

You are an important person—valuable in God's sight. And of all people, you should know who you are.

Notes
 1. *Bits and Pieces*, December 1977, p. 24.
 2. *Bits and Pieces*, January 1975, p. 1.
 3. For further study on God's grace, see *Free for the Taking* by Joseph R. Cooke (Old Tappan, N.J.: Revell, 1975).
 4. *Bits and Pieces*, October 1976, pp. 12-14.
 5. Tim LaHaye, *Spirit-Controlled Temperament* and *Transformed Temperaments* (Wheaton, Ill.: Tyndale, 1966, 1992, and 1971).
 6. Alex Haley, *Roots*, as condensed in *Reader's Digest*, April 1977, p. 153.

Chapter Eleven

SEXUAL MORALITY

———————————⟡———————————

Mike received Christ as a student in college. He began to study the Bible and grow in his faith. But when he graduated he lost interest and dropped out of all Christian activities. The reason? One minute in his apartment revealed the cause. His walls were plastered with pornographic pictures. He devoured the popular porno magazines. His mind lived in sexual fantasies in a make-believe world of pictures and dreams.

One evening the friend who had helped him grow in his faith back in college came to his apartment. After some discussion with Mike, he got up and began ripping the pictures off the wall. "This is rot!" he said. "It has captured you and is destroying your life!"

The whole process so shocked Mike that he came to his senses and began the process of breaking his slavery to pornography. Today Mike is a walking obediently with Christ, free from the mental entanglement of pornography.

You may ask, "How can you be so sure that this was the real cause? Mike may have overdone it, but isn't the human body a work of art to be enjoyed and admired?" But Mike was not merely enjoying an art form. His appetite for sexual fantasy was consuming his mental energies and increasingly preventing him from experiencing a healthy thought life. Believers like Mike must confront pornography as a moral issue.

Visual pornography is one of the issues of morality to which the Bible does not speak specifically or in great detail. Others are pornographic reading and the debated issue of male and female masturbation. How well we understand the more detailed biblical teaching on homosexuality and premarital and extramarital sex will determine how we view these other controversial issues.

We live in the age of freedom of expression and freedom of lifestyle. X-rated movies and magazines are available in every city. Legislation to control pornography has failed in most places. The sexual fiction of yesterday is the reality of today. Magazines displayed in supermarkets present articles featuring unmarried couples living together. Sex manuals advocate extramarital affairs. Fewer and fewer teenagers leave high school as virgins. Prime-time television flaunts homosexuality and infidelity.

Our chances of changing all this seem minuscule. But we must control the effect of this cultural pressure on the Christian community. When many theologians openly endorse popular immoral activities, confusion is inevitable. How can we know what is right?

First, we must be honest with what the Bible teaches. Interpreting the Bible in defense of our own prejudices can pervert its true teaching. We must not teach more or less than is actually there.

Then, we must be honest in our response to what the Bible teaches. Knowing Scripture is of little value unless we apply it to our lives. On issues about which the Bible does not directly speak, we must be honest with our conscience and motives. We live under the teaching *and* the implications of the teaching of Scripture.

Finally, we must be honest with our friends — those with whom immoral acts are committed as well as others who are directly or indirectly affected. None of us has the luxury of living only for ourselves. Others are always affected by our actions.

SEXUAL MORALS CLEARLY TAUGHT IN SCRIPTURE

We will examine first the issues that are clearly discussed in Scripture. With this foundation we can investigate other related issues. We must not be deluded into thinking that scriptural teaching does not apply today, or that the Bible is puritanical and simply does not fit today's free culture. If we begin treating God's Word in this way we will soon stop relying on it even as a guide for salvation.

EXTRAMARITAL SEX

In the New Testament, two basic words are used to describe sexual immorality: fornication (in Greek, *porneia*, from which we get the word *pornography*) and adultery (*moichos*).[1] Adultery refers to illicit sexual relations between a married person and any person other than his or her marriage partner. Fornication is a broader term, including premarital as well as extramarital sexual relationships. In some translations *porneia* is often translated as *immorality*.

One of the oldest directives on extramarital sex is found in the Ten Commandments: "You shall not commit adultery" (Exodus 20:14). Jesus reconfirmed this and other commands, saying, "You know the commandments, 'Do not murder, do not commit adultery . . .'" (Mark 10:19). In Paul's writings we read, "The works of the flesh are manifest, which are these: adultery, fornication, uncleanness, lasciviousness . . . of the which I tell you before, as I have also told you in time past, that they which do such things shall not inherit the kingdom of God" (Galatians 5:19-21, KJV). These and other passages of Scripture make it clear that the Bible forbids extramarital sex. Jesus referred to it as a sin when He told the woman caught in adultery, "Go, and sin no more" (John 8:11, KJV).

These statements are rather direct and abrupt. Many books written on this topic give detailed analyses of these passages. But clearly, the Bible teaches that extramarital sexual relationships are sin.

Premarital Sex

The Scriptures relating to adultery apply equally to premarital sex. But many in our society, while agreeing that extramarital sex constitutes a violation of marriage vows and the relationship between husband and wife, are much more liberal in their views on premarital sex. Some would argue that if love is present and marriage is intended, premarital sex is right.

The problem of teenage sexual activity and pregnancy is reaching almost epidemic proportions. A number of studies and surveys have reported on these trends. Regarding declining virginity rates among adolescents, the researchers' findings are fairly consistent: 50–70 percent of unmarried women between the ages of sixteen and twenty have had premarital sex; for unmarried men of the same ages, the number is around 80 percent.[2] Josh McDowell's extensive study on teenage sexual activity, done during the mid-eighties, reveals troubling statistics: 50 percent of sexually active nineteen-year-old males had their first sexual experience between the ages of eleven and thirteen; 87 percent of sexually active teens say they first had sex before age seventeen; 54 percent of teens in one survey had intercourse for the first time in a parent's home.[3]

McDowell's research on teenage pregnancy is equally grim. Over the last twenty years the percentage of illegitimate births by girls ages nineteen and under has increased from 15 to 51 percent. Sixty percent of these girls will be pregnant again in two years. Thirty-thousand under the age of fourteen become pregnant annually, 80 percent of whom drop out of school. Seventy percent of unwed pregnant teens will go on welfare, and of those who marry because of the pregnancy, 60 percent will be divorced in five years. As teen pregnancy rates have increased dramatically, the birth rate has fallen. Abortion as an alternative to giving birth has resulted in a 25 percent decline in birth rates between 1970 to 1984, and a doubling of the abortion rate during the same period. More than 400,000 teenage girls in the U.S. are having abortions annually.[4]

With increasing social pressure and explicit stimulation from television, books, and movies, the modern young adult lives in a constant barrage of sexual excitement. Add to this the concept that sex outside marriage is not sin, and the result is confused standards and fractured lives. McDowell comments,

> Are we really surprised to discover that 78 percent of all young people ages eighteen to twenty-nine believe there is nothing wrong with having sex before marriage as long as both people are emotionally ready? An overwhelmingly permissive attitude toward premarital sex prevails throughout our society. As a consequence, young people are paying the price for the recent sexual revolution which promised "joy, liberation, and good health" but in fact "delivered misery, disease, and even death."[5]

Society opposes premarital sex primarily on grounds of the danger of pregnancy and disease—not on particular moral grounds. Sex education and the free distribution of contraceptives have become the means of controlling these problems, from society's viewpoint. But we have no contraceptives for the conscience. The mark on those guilty of pre-marital sex carries a permanence that can never be forgot-ten or erased—especially if a pregnancy occurs.

Scripture commands us to "flee immorality" (1 Corinthians 6:18). Paul wrote that "this is the will of God, your sanctification; that is, that you abstain from sexual immorality" (1 Thessalonians 4:3). Solomon wrote that sexual intercourse should be kept within the bonds of marriage (Proverbs 5:3-20), and then warned that God sees all the ways of man and that "his own iniquities will capture the wicked" (5:21-22). "Keep your way from her [the adulteress]," he warned, "and do not go near the door of her house" (5:8).

The biblical view of marriage provides one of the great-est deterrents to premarital sex. Marriage is compared to the relationship of Christ to His body, the church (Ephesians 5:23-33). The Bible fully endorses sex in marriage and fully condemns it outside marriage: "Let marriage be held in honor among all, and let the marriage bed be undefiled; for fornicators and adulterers God will judge" (Hebrews 13:4). In marriage sex can be one of the highest forms of identifi-cation and relationship. But outside of marriage sex can be the least satisfying and least love-oriented aspect of a rela-tionship. God's idea for sex is a total giving of oneself to the marriage partner—a total commitment that is meaning-less outside the bonds of marriage.

But what if you have already violated these commands? Can you ever find fulfillment in marriage? Yes, you can be ful-filled, since God forgives. You can never change the past, and difficulties may result in your future relationships, but God is sufficient for any situation. Start where you are now and prepare for the future God has for you.

For a single person who will eventually marry, true hon-esty in relationships results from saving yourself for the man or woman God has chosen for you. Cling to biblical stand-ards of purity and morality at the beginning of your relationships and you will experience a healthy restraining influence on impure desires. Turning away from an unhealthy situation requires greater willpower than setting standards early and living by them. These same standards apply, of course, to those who will not marry and to those who are widowed or divorced.

Purity of life cuts across the grain of the pressure of society. God's power working within you provides the key, if you have yielded your life to Him.

HOMOSEXUALITY

The concept of freedom takes some strange turns. In both a secular and spiritual sense we cherish the innate feeling that we must be free to do anything we wish. We resist restraint because it seems oppressive.

In society's push for more freedom, sexual taboos that were once discussed only in medical writings are now openly exposed and advocated. The most prominent of these today is homosexuality, or, when applied to women, lesbianism. What does the Bible teach about homosexuality? One key passage relating to the issue is found in Romans 1:24-27:

> Therefore God gave them over in the lusts of their hearts to impurity, that their bodies might be dishonored among them. For they exchanged the truth of God for a lie, and worshipped and served the creature rather than the Creator, who is blessed forever. Amen.
>
> For this reason God gave them over to degrading passions; for their women exchanged the natural function for that which is unnatural, and in the same way also the men abandoned the natural function of the woman and burned in their desire towards one another, men with men committing indecent acts and receiving in their own persons the due penalty of their error.

This passage depicts people rejecting God and giving themselves to impurity. Their homosexuality is described as "degrading passions" and "unnatural," since the natural use of sex in marriage is between a man and a woman.

In a passage describing the unrighteous, Paul wrote, "Neither fornicators, nor idolaters, nor adulterers, nor effeminate, nor homosexuals, nor thieves, nor the covetous, nor drunkards, nor revilers, nor swindlers, shall inherit the kingdom of God" (1 Corinthians 6:9-10). This is a strong assertion, and it would be quite discouraging were it not for Paul's next statement: "And such were some of you; but you were washed, but you were sanctified, but you were justified in the name of the Lord Jesus Christ, and in the Spirit of our God" (verse 11). But again, this passage points out that homosexuality is sin, an unacceptable practice in God's eyes.

If you have homosexual tendencies or practices in your life, however, such a statement may ring hollow. You know that disentangling yourself from the burden of homosexual involvement involves more than a simple admonition.

Believers in Christ must face this problem with understanding and compassion. Experts have cited many biological and environmental reasons for a person becoming a homosexual, although these cannot form an excuse for actions that violate direct commands of Scripture.

But we must realize that homosexual drives are not simply "shut down" any more than normal sexual drives. In some ways, homosexuality resembles alcoholism in that in most cases the tendency is always present, even after extensive abstinence.

Whereas premarital and extramarital sex are sinful uses of a normal desire, homosexual activity results from an abnormal desire and is more difficult to rechannel into healthy and productive directions. The very root of the homosexual drive must be dealt with directly. Though illicit heterosexual acts can be eliminated by a decision of the will, homosexuals usually need special counsel and attention. Professional counsel from a pastor or a biblically oriented psychologist or counselor should be sought for help in dealing with homosexuality. Anyone can be helped and can have victory.

SUGGESTIONS FOR THOSE WITH A HISTORY OF ILLICIT SEX

The strong statements above may prove discouraging if you have a history of sexual experience in any of these areas. But be encouraged. God is interested in where you are in your life. Christ died for sin—all sin. You cannot change your personal history and God understands that. Start claiming the power and victory God offers. Try these practical suggestions:

1. Admit to yourself and to God that your actions have been sin. Confession is the key to forgiveness. "If we confess our sins, He is faithful and righteous to forgive us our sins and to cleanse us from all unrighteousness" (1 John 1:9).
2. Make a conscious decision of your will not to engage in this sexual sin again. You may feel this is impossible—and on your own it is. But God promises, "No temptation has overtaken you but such as is common to man; and God is faithful, who will not allow you to be tempted beyond what you are able, but with the temptation will provide the way of escape also, that you may be able to endure it" (1 Corinthians 10:13).
3. When problems or circumstances are particularly complex, obtain godly counsel. Even after the two steps above you may need to talk through the issues and get guidance on what to do next.
4. Since sexual activity requires another person's

involvement, you may need to ask forgiveness and make restitution. You should be careful about discussing premarital sexual experience you had prior to becoming a Christian with your husband or wife. If handled poorly it may do more harm than good. However, if there has been a violation of your marriage relationship, you may well need to confess this to your mate and ask his or her forgiveness. It would be unusual if your mate were not already suspicious and if there were not serious problems in your relationship that need attention.

5. Once you have done these things, accept God's total forgiveness and forget the past. God has forgiven you, but you will tend to dwell on the past as though you were not forgiven. Forget it, and move toward the future (see Psalm 103:8-14).

What follows is based on the fact that these categories of illicit sex discussed above are really sin and are prohibited by God.

THE ROOTS OF SEXUAL SIN

Sexual sin never begins by accident. People do not suddenly fall into an illicit sexual act simply by having an opportunity confront them. There is always some specific preparation. This preparation we call "pre-sexual" experience. Pre-sexual experiences are those experiences of mind and action that excite, train, or develop our sexual drives.

Not all pre-sexual experiences are wrong. They may prepare you for marriage. They may be relationships and experiences through which you learn to control and direct these God-given drives. On the other hand, some pre-sexual experiences build and contribute only to illicit sexual activity. Though an experience in itself may appear harmless, it leads directly to sin in due time. We can see this principle emphasized in the Bible.

Certain words used in Scripture relate to these experiences. Understanding them is the foundation for determining whether a sexual act or thought is sin.

1. *Sensuality* is the word usually translated in Scripture from the Greek word *aselgeia*, which denotes "excess," "absence of restraint," "indecency," and "shameless conduct."[6] The word is used in the passages listed below.

> For from within, out of the heart of men, proceed the evil thoughts and fornications . . . as well as . . . *sensuality*. (Mark 7:21-22, emphasis added)

> Now the deeds of the flesh are evident, which are: immorality, impurity, [and] *sensuality*. (Galatians 5:19, emphasis added)

> This I say therefore, and affirm together with the Lord, that you walk no longer just as the Gentiles also walk. . . . They, having become callous, have given themselves over to *sensuality*, for the practice of every kind of impurity with greediness. (Ephesians 4:17,19; emphasis added)

The dictionary definition for *sensual* includes these terms: "relating to or consisting in the gratification of the senses or the indulgence of appetite: fleshly; devoted to or preoccupied with the senses or appetites."[7]

In the passages above, the word *aselgeia* is rendered in other translations as *lasciviousness, licentiousness, debauchery,* and *lewdness.*

2. *Lusts, passions, desires,* or *cravings* are used in various modern translations for the Greek word *epithumia,* which is found in the passages that follow.

Now flee from youthful *lusts*, and pursue righteousness. (2 Timothy 2:22, emphasis added)

Abstain from fleshly *lusts*, which wage war against the soul. (1 Peter 2:11, emphasis added)

For all that is in the world, the *lust* of the flesh and the *lust* of the eyes and the boastful pride of life, is not from the Father, but is from the world. (1 John 2:16, emphasis added)

Lust is defined as "intense sexual desire" and "an intense longing."[8]

God's concern for our lives extends beyond the obvious acts of immorality. The above passages indicate that improper thoughts and desires later lead to sexual sin.

THE GRAY AREAS OF MORALITY

In discussing sexual issues that are not specifically listed in Scripture, keep in mind that certain pre-sexual experiences easily lead to sensuality or lust.

OUR THOUGHTS

The battle for sexual purity always begins in the mind. What we constantly think of, we ultimately do. We fill our minds with good or evil, the pure or the impure, right or wrong. Many believers harbor both in the inner recesses of their thought life.

Overt sexual sin is conceived in the mind, developed in various pre-sexual experiences, and finally becomes a reality when given opportunity. Not only is the resulting immorality sin—the impure thoughts, too, are sin. Jesus' words in the Sermon on the Mount are frequently quoted in this regard: "You have heard that it was said, 'You shall not commit adultery'; but I say to you, that everyone who looks on a woman to lust for her has committed adultery with her already in his heart" (Matthew 5:27-28). Do not get confused and say, "Since I have already sinned in my heart, I might as well sin in the body." These sins are not the same! One is the sin of the mind, and in the mind only one person sins. The other is a sin of the mind and the body, and in the body, two people sin. In the mind, there is no physical union. In the body the two have come to know each other in an irreversible way. Note in verse 28 Jesus mentions not just looking, but looking "to lust." This involves an active desire imagining a sexual union or contact.

God knows all our thoughts. "For the word of God is . . . able to judge the thoughts and intentions of the heart. And there is no creature hidden from His sight, but all things are open and laid bare to the eyes of Him with whom we have to do" (Hebrews 4:12-13).

Paul said that the Spirit-controlled Christian in spiritual battle is "taking *every* thought captive to the obedience of Christ" (2 Corinthians 10:5, emphasis added). And Peter said, "Gird your minds for action. . . . Do not be conformed to the former lusts which were yours in your ignorance" (1 Peter 1:13-14). We cannot prevent every impure thought from entering the mind, but we do control the thoughts that remain and develop.

God gives us ways to develop a pure mind and thought life, since "we have the mind of Christ" (1 Corinthians 2:16). "Be transformed by the renewing of your mind" (Romans 12:2). This renewing is a continuing, repetitive process. Today's victory will not ensure winning tomorrow's battle.

To control the thoughts we must fill the mind with the right things: "Whatever is true, whatever is honorable, whatever is right, whatever is pure, whatever is lovely, whatever is of good repute, if there is any excellence and if anything worthy of praise, let your mind *dwell* on these things" (Philippians 4:8, emphasis added).

The most powerful means of filling and controlling the mind is memorizing Scripture. As you memorize various portions of the Bible, your mind will turn to them when temptation occurs. If you have never memorized Scripture on a regular basis, let me encourage you to try it.[9]

One of the verses that has been a great help to me in controlling my thought life is Proverbs 16:3: "Commit thy works unto the Lord and thy thoughts shall be established" (KJV). Modern versions translate the word *thoughts* as *plans*. Both are related to the mind. What you *do* affects your thought life. And what you *think* controls what you do.

Our Eyes

What our eyes see and read produces and controls the vast majority of our thoughts. Jesus taught that the eye is the lamp of the body (Matthew 6:22-23) and that if the eye is bad, the body will be full of darkness. This truth describes more than a physical fact. It refers to what the eye allows to enter the mind.

The apostle John warned about "the lust of the eyes" (1 John 2:16). Solomon wrote, "Let your eyes look directly ahead, and let your gaze be fixed straight in front of you. *Watch* the path of your feet, and all your ways will be established" (Proverbs 4:25-26, emphasis added). Solomon also said, "Give me your heart, my son, and let your *eyes* delight in my ways. For a harlot is a deep pit, and an adulterous woman is a narrow well" (23:26-27, emphasis added).

The eyes are the gate to the mind. Whenever possible, we must guard what they see.

Pornography

In the United States and around the world, pornography is big business. Millions, perhaps billions, of dollars are spent yearly on many forms of pornography. And as society continues to move further from a Judeo-Christian understanding of morality, other restraints will be removed.

Cases in many law courts have shown that the definition of pornography is extremely difficult, if not impossible. More than a decade ago, the publisher of one pornographic magazine responded this way when asked about federal and state laws on obscene materials: "All such laws are unjust! The First Amendment of the Constitution guarantees complete freedom of speech and press, and that covers everything. In 20 years all laws against so-called obscenity will be wiped from the books!"[10]

For our purposes, we will define pornography as any pictures, magazines, books, television programs, or movies that stimulate a person's sexual drive to sensuality or lust.

Within this definition are two types of pornography—visual and written. Visual pornography includes the many popular magazines with pictures of naked women or men or of people in provocative poses, and the many sexually oriented movies. Christians may think these would never become a problem for them, but many of them get "hooked" on R- and X-rated movies and this devastates their spiritual lives.

As I talked with one man who was battling a whole range of sexual sins and was just beginning to overcome them after two years of discouragement, I referred to pornography as a "gray" area. He stiffened and blurted out, "You aren't calling pornography a gray area, are you? It's sin." He knew the part pornography had played in his downfall. He even kept a record of when he "slipped" by dwelling on movie ads in the newspaper.

Especially for one who battles masturbation or illicit sex, all provocative material must be avoided, because it generates great problems in the thought life. Even one who does not normally scrutinize visual pornography can easily wander to a newsstand and begin paging through the readily available magazines, thereby directing his mind to impure thoughts.

As for written pornography, many best-selling books appeal to readers because of their vivid descriptions of sexual acts. Even some "good" literature can present problems in the mind of a Christian.

Unfortunately, once these sexual images are formed they tend to remain imprinted in our minds. While traveling on an airplane not long ago I strolled around during the flight and found a discarded book. I opened it and began to read, and soon learned that it contained illicit sex accounts. I knew I should put it down. But I didn't until I had read one incident. Even today that image still invades my mind and disturbs me. Once implanted, such thoughts are difficult, though not impossible, to erase.

If you keep pornographic or questionable books around your house or where you work, burn them. Don't let them remain to tempt you.

But what about the student or worker who must live in the midst of someone else's pornography? The man mentioned earlier who stressed that pornography was a sin had developed an interest through other people's material. We cannot dictate the choices of others.

The only alternative is to exercise self-discipline and *never* allow yourself the partial freedom to "look just a little." There is no halfway point. Compromise will not work.

You can also try diplomatically to have pornography removed. A good relationship with a roommate or coworker can provide the basis for telling him that the pictures are offensive. If not, your only choice is to spend time elsewhere, or, if that is impossible, to control your eyes. God knows your circumstances and will also guard your mind.

Some who read these ideas may laugh and consider them simplistic, puritanical, and cloistered. After all, a person must live in the world as it really is. Christians cannot be so sheltered and naive that they don't relate to real people, can they?

But Paul wrote, "I want you to be wise in what is good, and innocent in what is evil" (Romans 16:19). We can discuss these things under all guises of sophistication, but we know the spiritual danger encountered when sexual looseness invades our minds and bodies. "Can a man take fire in his bosom, and his clothes not be burned? Or can a man walk on hot coals and his feet not be scorched? So is the one who goes in to his neighbor's wife" (Proverbs 6:27-29). We must not play with fire that threatens our lives—both spiritually and physically. The Bible tells us, "It is disgraceful even to speak of the things which are done by [unbelievers] in secret" (Ephesians 5:12).

Unquestionably, pornography can control the mind. If we wish to guard our minds as God's Word teaches, we must resist personal indulgence in pornography.

MASTURBATION[11]

Several years ago I was helping a college student grow spiritually. When we discussed witnessing or sharing his faith he constantly appeared defeated. I could not determine why he was unable to openly and publicly identify with Christ. Finally, one day he shared that he had a problem with masturbation and simply could not honestly share his faith with others when he was unable to get victory in this area of his life. I began to counsel him on the problem. Yet he never gained victory. His life slid further and further into carnal behavior with almost no discernible identification with Christ.

You could respond to the account of this student in several ways. You could contend that his problem was guilt over something that was not sin at all. You might say that if I had described masturbation to him as a normal, healthy sexual experience he would have continued to grow in his faith. Some may say masturbation should be encouraged. Others may view it as being wrong, but say that a legalistic approach to the problem is more damaging than helpful.

Whatever your response, it is likely to be influenced by your personal experience with masturbation. And if statistics are correct, a majority of men and women have had some experience. Some estimate that more than 90 percent of all adult males practice or have practiced masturbation. For women the percentage is now probably over 50 percent. The practice is becoming more common for women due to the greater availability of instruction books and much greater public encouragement by other women.

Most nonbelievers and many believers do not consider masturbation a problem. Certainly they do not feel it is sin, but rather that it becomes a problem only when it is an obsession and a total psychological substitute for normal sex relations.

Many myths about masturbation fill older Catholic and Protestant writings on the topic. Some of these myths are that it is physically harmful, that it will damage one's sexual ability in marriage, or that it will make one emotionally disturbed. These myths were primarily scare tactics and had little basis in fact.

No specific Scriptures speak directly to this issue of masturbation. Some call attention to Genesis 38:8-10 and 1 Corinthians 6:9-10. I agree with Herbert J. Miles[12] that these passages do not speak of masturbation.

Yet the Bible does give guidelines that will allow you to decide if masturbation is sin for you. Consider these observations:

1. Recall the definition of *sensuality* and *lust*: "gratification of the senses or the indulgence of appetite; devoted to or preoccupied with the senses" and "intense sexual desire." Masturbation definitely fits these definitions (see Galatians

5:19). Can you practice masturbation without engaging in sensuality or lust?

2. The next test is that of your *thought life*. Jesus said, "I say to you, that everyone who looks on a woman to lust for her has committed adultery with her already in his heart" (Matthew 5:28). When a person practices masturbation, what is in his or her mind? Can a person practice masturbation without imagining a sexual act or at least sensual pictures? How do you feel? If you practice masturbation, can your mind remain pure?

3. Next consider the sanctity and intent of the sexual relationship in marriage. Without question, masturbation is an attempt to experience the same sensations meant to be experienced in marriage. It is a *substitute for the real thing*—a fake, a fabrication, and a deceit.

4. Also, masturbation is *totally self-centered*. One characteristic of self-centeredness is self-indulgence. Paul described the way of life of one controlled by Satan, saying, "We too all formerly lived in the lusts of our flesh; indulging the desires of the flesh and of the mind" (Ephesians 2:3).

5. Finally, masturbation can put us in *bondage*. When a person is controlled by a fleshly indulgence, he sins. "Therefore do not let sin reign in your mortal body that you should obey its lusts" (Romans 6:12). Paul also said, "All things are lawful for me, but not all things are profitable. All things are lawful for me, but *I will not be mastered* by anything" (1 Corinthians 6:12, emphasis added). Are you in bondage to masturbation?

Consider the above five statements to determine if masturbation is sin for you.

You may feel that all of this is fine theoretically, but that it doesn't help you overcome masturbation. In fact, you may have just been launched on a further guilt trip. So it would be unfair to end the discussion at this point without giving some practical guidelines to help in overcoming it.

First we will define the limits of our discussion and some aspects of the human sex drive. All of this discussion focuses on men and women eighteen years of age and older. In early and middle adolescence many things happen sexually that are part of the growing process. In this context masturbation frequently occurs. This may be regarded as either right or wrong, but the process of handling it is different. These suggestions pertain to mature men and women who because of age and mental and emotional maturity can make rational and spiritual decisions based on God's direction for their lives. Whatever one's history of masturbation in adolescence, each adult assumes responsibility for his actions today. Personal history does affect the present circumstances and the difficulty of changing — but it cannot be an excuse.

The sex drive is a normal, God-given part of any healthy man or woman. To be ashamed of it is to doubt God's goodness to us. To misuse it is to thwart God's intended joy for us. God created us with many drives and desires that we can develop or misuse. As one of these, the sex drive energizes or destroys relationships, depending on its control and application.

Significant differences in the sex drive exist between men and women. A man's sex drive develops strongly in adolescence and demands release. Beginning in adolescence (the onset of puberty), a man's body produces sperm and stores them in seminal vesicles. When they are filled, the sex drive increases and demands a release of these fluids. The male sex drive is biological as well as psychological and emotional. His drive becomes even greater when aroused by sight or thought, and responds readily and strongly to visual stimulus or to touch.

God designed the male's body to handle this in a natural way. The seminal fluid is naturally released by means of nocturnal or night emissions. When this first occurs in puberty, it may cause a boy embarrassment as though it were bedwetting. Parents must explain that this is a natural process—and, in fact, encourage it. When there are no nocturnal emissions, the necessary release likely is occurring through sex relations or masturbation. From a biological standpoint, masturbation is *not* necessary.

In men masturbation develops almost automatically because of the combination of his sex drive and the external nature of his sex organs. Therefore, if it is to be avoided, it must be a choice—a decision of the will.

The sex drive in a woman differs significantly. A woman's biological system does not automatically build up a drive that demands release. In fact, it generally must be awakened from within and requires a much stronger integration of mind and body. A man almost "naturally" turns to masturbation for release, but a woman generally must learn masturbation or be taught. However, once awakened, masturbation may become even more captivating and controlling for a woman.

A woman is stimulated sexually more by touch than by sight. In the past, women rarely viewed pornographic stimuli. However, today women are exposed to so much more visual stimuli that, when coupled with previous masturbation or sexual experience, they become sexually aroused. It is more difficult for a woman to develop a strong habit of masturbation, and also more difficult to break it. Herbert Miles says, "Since a young woman does not have a strong sex drive demanding release, masturbation would be using for individual secret pleasure that which God created for social and spiritual purposes in the one-flesh relationship of marriage. The female orgasm is not just a biological procedure; rather, it is a love response and expression to the one loved, the husband."[13]

Masturbation is a common problem. We must not be afraid to talk about it and to get help to overcome it. Men and women find the habit equally oppressive and are seeking help in overcoming the problem. Compassion, not condemnation, must be the response.

Many persons, including Christians, who say that masturbation is acceptable and even desirable ignore the evidence to the contrary. In their excellent book dealing with the issue, Walter and Ingrid Trobisch say, "Our impression is rather that the more the sexual taboos are breaking down, the more masturbation becomes a problem for individuals. The rational conclusion that objectively no harm is done evidently does not quench the subjective feeling of shameful personal defeat. In spite of all the soothing arguments in favor of [masturbation], few are really happy with it."[14] Later they say that masturbation "is not a sickness. It is a symptom, a sign of a deeper problem. . . . Usually deep down, there is a feeling of dissatisfaction with oneself and with one's life, which one tries to overcome in a short moment of pleasure."[15]

My conclusion is that masturbation should not be a part of a believer's life. First Corinthians 6:18-20, Galatians 5:19 and 1 Thessalonians 4:3-7 speak to the issue of using our bodies properly in sex. Paul said, "This is the will of God . . . that each of you know how to possess his own vessel in sanctification and honor, not in lustful passions, like the Gentiles who do not know God" (1 Thessalonians 4:3-5). Though we may not settle all arguments about masturbation being sin, we cannot deny that it results from lust and passion. But in the freedom of God's grace we may *choose* to do that which is holy and right in God's sight.

PRACTICAL SUGGESTIONS FOR OVERCOMING MASTURBATION
There is no cookbook formula for victory over masturba-

tion. What helps one person may not help another. But these guidelines listed below can help many.

1. *Personal conviction.* Do you really believe that masturbation is wrong from a biblical perspective? Do you believe specifically that it is wrong for you? Study the biblical view of sex and marriage to develop the conviction that God designed sex exclusively for marriage. Then study such passages as Job 31:1, Proverbs 6:25-33, Matthew 15:19, 1 Corinthians 6:15-18, Galatians 5:19, and 1 Thessalonians 4:3-7.

2. *Decision.* You must decide that you really want victory over masturbation and are willing to work at it. When counseling one man about this I asked another counselor how he helped people in this area. He immediately asked, "Does he really want victory? If he doesn't you can't help him." The flesh does not want victory, but the mind must override the flesh. Decide that you *need* victory even when it is hard to want it.

3. *Prayer and God's power.* A basic step to victory is confession in prayer. We must admit to God that masturbation is sin for us, and claim His forgiveness (1 John 1:9). From 1 Corinthians 10:13 we can claim God's deliverance from temptation. He does promise victory. We can ask Him for this victory. But there is a wrong time to pray—when desire for masturbation is at its height and you are about to fall. Praying may focus your mind on it even more. Prayer is most effective early in the temptation process. Later, only your will can deliver you.

4. *Your mind.* Masturbation begins in the mind. The real battle in pre-sexual activities takes place in the mind. Do not allow your thoughts to *dwell* on sexual things, and your victory is almost assured.

5. *Your eyes.* Keep your eyes from pornographic material and anything that stimulates you sexually. I do not mean you cannot look at another person or accidentally glance at sensual things. But dwelling on these things gives the oppor-

tunity for sexual desire to develop. Just before writing these lines, I was on an airplane and was glancing through a popular news magazine. One page featured a picture of a woman in a revealing bathing suit. I was inclined to prolong the look by "reading" the rest of the page. I had to force myself to turn the page immediately.

6. *Avoiding tempting circumstances*. Anyone who is trapped by masturbation knows that certain circumstances almost always surround the act. A person is usually alone, frequently at night, and is often physically tired. Know your own circumstances and work at avoiding them or altering them to be less tempting, such as going elsewhere and talking to someone else to redirect your mind. The problem is that when the desire becomes great a person begins planning to be alone to do it.

7. *Your will.* Ultimately masturbation will be avoided when you deliberately choose not to do it. Techniques, tricks, and diversions will not prevent it if you do not decide to resist the temptation. You cannot stop fleeting thoughts of the mind, but you can prevent physical actions. As one person expressed it, "When I really want it, I would drive through a concrete wall or run over my grandmother." No habit breaks easily. But resisting once will make it easier to resist a second time.

8. *Other outlets*. Vigorous physical exercise will help dissipate sexual tensions and drive. Deep concerns actively directed toward other people can frequently divert the mind from dwelling on self-centered issues that lead to masturbation. Helping others spiritually provides a restraint, since you will frequently be helping them overcome various sins in their own lives. A man who was desperately battling masturbation, and who had finally become addicted to both pornography and massage parlors, told me that at one time when he had consistent victory for a month, he had his first nocturnal emission in two years. The body *will* adjust and compensate.

9. *Help from others*. As long as masturbation and its related activities are a private affair, motivation must come totally from within. Frequently, sharing your problem with a trusted friend or counselor can give the extra motivation you need to talk about the issues and make specific commitments to change. Ask your friend or counselor to check up on you. You need some type of objective evaluation rather than saying, "Well, I am doing fairly well," or "I slipped a couple of times," when that may be quite different from reality. The pressure of an outside influence and commitment can help you significantly.

10. *Total victory*. Is total victory really possible? Yes, it is. One person said, "If I didn't think I could have total victory, I couldn't survive." One woman shared frankly, "I eventually stopped—again, not without struggle and stumbling, but I stopped. I wanted God's Spirit more than I wanted transient physical titillation, and, over and above that, I began to see that abstinence made sense in terms of optimal preparation for *real* sharing with a *real* person."[16]

Does victory for every person mean that masturbation never again happens? Not necessarily. We do not reach sinless perfection in this life, and will always battle the flesh. But, if you fall to masturbation, it will be temporary and incidental, not a practiced or planned relapse. Many have victory for months and years. It is possible.

11. *Time and failure*. Deeply ingrained habits do not change in days. The process of gaining victory over masturbation takes both time and effort. Times of failure in the process of change are almost inevitable. But no failure is final. Although some people can make a decision one day to stop and never do it again, they are in the minority. Most people will see increasingly longer periods of victory.

When you fail, confess it and keep going in your attempt to overcome the habit. Although you will battle discouragement when you fail, treat it as discouragement from any other sin. Don't let discouragement defeat you. Remember that an alcoholic does not easily overcome his habit—and even when he has stopped drinking there is still a desire to drink. Masturbation is much the same. It forms a similar hold on you and requires the same discipline to break the habit. Keep trying no matter how much failure you may experience. God can give you ultimate victory.

12. *Guilt*. When a person sins, guilt often sets in—even after confession to God. If we have confessed to God (1 John 1:9), we have no real guilt before Him. But the guilt remains in our minds and feelings. Although we cannot live continuously under the burden of guilt, it does serve the purpose of keeping us sensitive to sin and aware of our weakness and dependence on God.

The Trobisches deal with the process of time, failure, and overcoming guilt, and tell of a girl who worked through the gradual overcoming process. "It would not have helped her if we had tried to convince her that there was nothing wrong with it. She felt base, inferior and dirty. We worked first of all with her on the prolongation of the intervals while at the same time we tackled her problem of loneliness. . . . Gradually it became more and more infrequent and today she is completely free from it. But it took almost a year."[17]

Masturbation in marriage falls in the same category as described above, but to discuss this more fully is outside the scope of this work and belongs more properly in a Christian marriage manual.

In summary, masturbation is an indication of deeper needs. It may be that one's relationship with God has never been started or developed. Perhaps other feelings or problems have never been dealt with properly. Even with the many secular assurances that masturbation is acceptable, most people think like a woman who told the Trobisches, "I had feared one thing—that the answer would repeat what one can read everywhere nowadays: 'Keep on doing it and stop worrying. It won't do you any harm. It might even be beneficial to your sexual development.' All I know is that such advice does not help me because it contradicts a voice within me. . . . The fact that you did not okay it was the first help. . . ."[18]

What about you? What does your conscience tell you? What does your conscience say as you read the various Scriptures on God's purpose in sex and His plan for your body? Be bold. Be willing to do what you determine is right from conscience and the Bible.

AFFECTIONS AND LOVE
The focus of your affection will eventually affect your body. Divorce cases of the past were sometimes based on "alienation of affections." It is a seldom used phrase now, but a very real concept. Although many would not consider affections a matter of sexual morality, they do strongly influence pre-sexual experiences.

Affection is not always lust. A person can be strongly drawn to one of the opposite sex on other than a sexual basis. We can genuinely like and appreciate others in a very healthy way. But for married people, there may come a point when we see our affections being directed away from our mate to another.

The process begins with looks and expressions of appreciation. Next follows lengthy conversation of a "deep" nature, often about personal feelings. Thoughts of this person as a sexual partner in comparison to one's mate begin to develop. Then there is occasional touching and physical contact. Finally, total affection and love is transferred from one's mate to the other person.

The process and sequence may vary, but the result is the same—broken marriages and divorce. In most of these cases the full sexual process from illicit sex thoughts to actual adultery occurs.

The Scripture warns, "You shall not covet your neighbor's wife" (Exodus 20:17). Guard your affections and love. It is possible to fall in love with anyone. Do not allow yourself to find emotional satisfaction in a relationship outside your marriage.

The same process can occur among those who are single. This process can lead to a God-directed marriage. On the other hand, the same sequence can be fed primarily by sensual desire without an appreciation of true love involving sacrifice and commitment.

THE DATING GAME

Dating is a modern custom. The practice is not found in the Bible. It is not contrary to the Bible, but simply was not practiced in biblical times. Yet in our culture dating for fun and for determining a potential marriage partner has become a way of life.

Many persons equate dating with sexual relations. For most Christians, though, dating precedes marriage as a way of developing relationships. What kind of physical involvement is right and proper in dating? Here again we will focus on the young adult age group — those for whom dating constitutes, to some degree, a search for a marriage partner.

Although the Bible is silent on dating, it speaks forcibly on sensuality and lust. We are to avoid arousing sexual desires that cannot be rightly fulfilled outside marriage. You may feel that a person would have to be dead or totally insensitive to live within this boundary as engagement and marriage approach. But God can refocus our thinking and actions when true, sacrificial love develops. And when a couple has their focus on honoring God and keeping their bodies for marriage, they experience a new perspective and power.

As the commitment of engaged couples to marriage grows, restraint becomes difficult. Therefore, let us consider a few ideas on dating and the physical relationship. You must determine the precise boundaries for yourself in these areas, based on scriptural teaching on sensuality and lust.

1. *Past sexual experience.* If you have had sexual experience, you need to determine additional restraints for yourself since you have been sexually awakened and are more susceptible to stimulation. In fact, if you have recently become a Christian and have had sexual experience, you may want to totally forego dating for some time while you develop a godly perspective toward dating and marriage.

2. *Double-dating.* Restrict single dating in the early stages of developing a relationship. Double-dating affords extra protection from a focus on the physical.

3. *Relationship sequence.* Work on developing spiritual and intellectual relationships first. Plenty of emotion fills these relationships even without physical contact.

4. *Early physical contact.* When a couple moves to physical contact, the focus of their relationship undergoes a drastic change. If this occurs in the early stages of a relationship, spiritual and intellectual communication becomes stifled by the physical. It is best if there is *no* physical contact (such as embracing and kissing) in casual dating in the early part of even a serious relationship. Do not allow physical involvement to suppress the development of intellectual and spiritual closeness, for these provide the lasting basis for a good marriage.

5. *Petting and necking.* When hand-holding moves to embracing and kissing, a totally new dimension of the relationship develops. It would seem unnatural not to express premarital love in some embracing

and kissing—but what is the limit? We could say, "Don't kiss or embrace until marriage." But the Bible does not say that.

Problems arise with *prolonged* embracing, kissing, and caressing whose natural outcome is sexual intercourse. We can argue about precise limits and definitions, but each of us knows when the turning point from expression to arousal occurs in our body. This appears to be the biblical limit as defined by the concept of defrauding and sensuality (see 1 Thessalonians 4:3-7). Write down these standards for yourself, and then discuss them with your dating partner and set limits and standards acceptable to both of you as the relationship moves toward marriage.

6. *Starting over*. If you are already beyond these limits, you must begin again. Usually you must go all the way back to no physical contact whatsoever as you rebuild a proper foundation. Don't endanger your future marriage by living with the status quo, if your conscience has convicted you about your conduct.

7. *Self-control*. Self-control may be the greatest asset to successful courtship and marriage. True love honestly seeks the other person's good. It is strength under control. It is intensity with restraint. In handling the sex drive in courtship, self-control will build trust and self-esteem rather than embarrassment and suspicion. Don't cash in the greatest investment you can make in marriage—giving your total self to another.

These ideas may sound contrary to current social views and perhaps to your personal experience. But believers in Christ are given different standards to live by.

KEY HELPS IN KEEPING MORALLY PURE

HOLINESS

Holiness of life has become almost extinct in evangelical conversation and teaching. Yet we are commanded, "Like the Holy One who called you, be holy yourselves also in all your behavior; because it is written, 'You shall be holy for I am holy'" (1 Peter 1:15-16).

Scripture teaches two aspects of holiness. The first is our holy, righteous standing before God. This can be true only as a person becomes a Christian by believing in Jesus Christ as his or her personal Savior. Only in salvation can we enter a holy standing before God. Our becoming holy in this sense occurred through Christ's death and resurrection.

Paul wrote, "Although you were formerly alienated and hostile in mind, engaged in evil deeds, yet He has now reconciled you in His fleshly body through death, in order to present you before Him holy and blameless and beyond reproach" (Colossians 1:21-22). The basic meaning of holiness here is to be set apart to God for salvation. If you do not possess this salvation, you cannot have the power to overcome sin and to know the second aspect of holiness, which is personal and relates to our conduct: "Do you not know that you are a temple of God, and that the Spirit of God dwells in you? If any man destroys the temple of God, God will destroy him, for *the temple of God is holy, and that is what you are*" (1 Corinthians 3:16-17, emphasis added).

Paul said, "For God has not called us for the purpose of impurity, but in sanctification [holiness]" (1 Thessalonians 4:7). We have a personal responsibility to pursue holiness, not to earn our salvation but to live pure lives.[19] We are to "cleanse ourselves from all defilement of flesh and spirit, perfecting holiness in the fear of God" (2 Corinthians 7:1).

God desires for you to live a holy life. What is your desire? "Blessed are the pure in heart, for they shall see God" (Matthew 5:8).

PERSONAL WALK WITH GOD

Many people are assured of their salvation, but fail to live holy lives because of a weak daily relationship with God. To strive for personal holiness and purity on our own power without daily fellowship with Christ is like trying to put toothpaste back in the tube—great effort with no results. We need regular, personal fellowship with Christ. A daily time of reading the Scriptures, meditating on them, and praying is a Christian's lifeline. A person can live in sin and still have a regular devotional life—but he will be miserable in so doing.

If you need help in developing a personal devotional or quiet time, take five or ten minutes a day to receive life-giving infusions of His Word and His fellowship. It will change your life, and give you power to resist sin.[20]

SCRIPTURE MEMORY

Since sin usually begins in the mind, we need to fill our minds with what is good. And what is better than God's Word? I urge you to begin memorizing Scripture on a regular basis.[21]

DECISION AND SELF-CONTROL

Those who glide through life doing what comes naturally will never develop character and depth. All the knowledge you can accumulate will never change your life unless you exercise willpower and self-control. The direct commands of Scripture need to be taken seriously. But obedience means self-control. "Watch over your heart with *all diligence*, for from it flow the springs of life" (Proverbs 4:23, emphasis added). "*Choose* for yourselves today whom you will serve" (Joshua 24:15, emphasis added). "If you love Me, you will *keep* My commandments" (John 14:15, emphasis added).

As you attempt to live a holy life, make firm decisions and learn to control your desires. These virtues will then permeate every area of your life.

Fellowship

None of us can stand alone. With all the bravado of self-sufficiency and independence thrust upon us by our society, deep inside we are weak and we desperately need others. "Two are better than one because they have a good return for their labor. For if either of them falls, the one will lift up his companion. But woe to the one who falls when there is not another to lift him up" (Ecclesiastes 4:9-10). In matters of morality and sin, close personal fellowship forms one of our best protections. We need people who are concerned enough to probe to find out how we are doing spiritually. Do you have anyone who is that close to you?

When we are in sin, we unfortunately avoid fellowship with other Christians. That is when we must force ourselves to relate and to share openly. Consider Hebrews 10:24-25:

> Let us consider how to stimulate one another to love and good deeds, not forsaking our own assembling together, as is the habit of some, but encouraging one another, and all the more, as you see the day drawing near.

We do need the church, the local body of believers. Many times the influence of a local church on the personal conduct of its members can seem legalistic. Yet, many need precisely that—a restraint to keep them from associations and activities that would tempt and lead them to sin. Don't live your faith in isolation from other believers. Be part of a body of believers. Find close personal fellowship in that body. The fellowship of believers will protect, encourage, and nourish you.

AVOID COMPROMISING SITUATIONS

Many believers treat temptation recklessly, seeing how far they can go without falling. You know yourself—your weaknesses, your hang-ups, your private temptations, and your susceptible areas. When you are aware of places, circumstances, or people that put you in jeopardy of sin and induce temptation, only one answer can suffice: Avoid it! Run! Get away! No matter what the pressure or social consequences, adopt the aviator's smartest move when encountering a storm—a 180-degree turn. "Do not enter the path of the wicked, and do not proceed in the way of evil men. Avoid it, do not pass by it; turn away from it and pass on" (Proverbs 4:14-15). Better to be a coward and to live to fight another day than to fight and fall. In fact, real courage is to run rather than to "save face" and stay.

BIBLE STUDY ON SEX, LOVE, AND MARRIAGE

Take time to study some of the Bible references given in this chapter to discover their truths on your own. Study especially the topics of love, sex, and marriage.

On love, use a concordance to find references to it in the Bible. Then look up the passages and categorize them into God's love, our love for God, our love for others, and marriage love. Study in particular John 13:34-35, 21:15-17; 1 Corinthians 13; and 1 John.

On sex, study the book of Proverbs, categorizing verses relating to sex. Also study the passages used in this chapter, especially 1 Corinthians 7.

On marriage, study Proverbs 31, 1 Corinthians 7, Ephesians 5, and 1 Peter 3. There are also several helpful prepared Bible studies on marriage. Your ultimate source of direction should be the Word of God, His Spirit, and your conscience, rather than other people's opinion.

CHANGING YOUR LIFE

Habits die slowly—especially the ones we enjoy. As you honestly examine yourself, you may see the need to totally repattern your thoughts and life in the area of sexual morality. This takes time, work, and patience. Be willing to go through the process of change. Build new habits to serve you.

PHYSICAL AND MENTAL WELL-BEING

People are far more susceptible to entrapment by sin when they are down physically, emotionally, and mentally. One key counterattack to temptation is to keep healthy physically by proper eating, rest, and exercise.

Likewise, keep yourself mentally fit. Keep your mind active with learning new things, as well as personal and vocational development. When your mind goes into neutral, the thought life begins to crumble and questionable amusements begin to take over. Your mind is never empty. The only question is what fills it.

Do yourself a favor. Keep healthy, physically and mentally.

FAILURE AND FORGIVENESS

Failure is the mark of a human. Forgiveness is the mark of God. James said, "For we all stumble in many ways" (James 3:2). Paul described his own struggle this way: "The good that I wish, I do not do; but I practice the very evil that I do not wish" (Romans 7:19). Yet Paul taught that we can know victory in Christ.

In dealing with the moral areas of your life, you will see some failure, but God is greater than your failure. Satan wants you to become discouraged so that you give up and fully enter into sin. God wants you to simply confess your sin and "make no [further] provision for the flesh" (Romans

13:14). *The Living Bible* paraphrases this entire verse, "Ask the Lord Jesus Christ to help you live as you should, and don't make plans to enjoy evil."

Moral victory is yours in Christ.

Notes

1. W. E. Vine, *An Expository Dictionary of New Testament Words*, vol. II, p. 125, and vol. I, p. 32.
2. Statistics were taken from three sources: Josh McDowell and Dick Day, *Why Wait? What You Need to Know About the Teen Sexuality Crisis* (San Bernadino, Calif.: Here's Life, 1987), p. 21; Nell Bernstein, "Learning to Love," *Mother Jones* January/February 1995, p. 49; Vern L. Bullough and Bonnie Bullough, "Premarital Sexuality," *Human Sexuality, An Encyclopedia* (New York: Garland Publishing, 1994), p. 484.
3. McDowell and Day, *Why Wait?*, p. 21-24.
4. McDowell and Day, *Why Wait?*, p. 21-24.
5. McDowell and Day, *Why Wait?*, p. 25.
6. Vine, *Expository Dictionary*, vol. II, p. 310.
7. *Webster's New Collegiate Dictionary*, p. 1056.
8. *Webster's New Collegiate Dictionary*, p. 685.
9. The Navigators' *Topical Memory System* presents a practical, simple plan for beginning Scripture memory. Published by NavPress, it is available from Christian bookstores.
10. O. K. Armstrong, "A Victory over the Smut Peddlers," Reader's Digest, February 1967, p. 147.
11. I recommend a book by Robert Daniels on the subject of sexual obsession/dysfunction in men. It is planned for 1997 release by Crossway Books.
12. Herbert J. Miles, *Sexual Understanding Before Marriage* (Grand Rapids, Mich.: Zondervan, 1971).
13. Miles, *Sexual Understanding*, p. 175.
14. From *My Beautiful Feeling* by Walter and Ingrid Trobisch, © 1976 by Editions Trobisch, Baden-Baden, Germany, and used by permission of InterVarsity Press; pp. 8-9.
15. Trobisch, *My Beautiful Feeling*, p. 18.
16. Trobisch, *My Beautiful Feeling*, p. 116.
17. Trobisch, *My Beautiful Feeling*, pp. 80-81.
18. Trobisch, *My Beautiful Feeling*, pp. 21.
19. See also *The Pursuit of Holiness* by Jerry Bridges (Colorado Springs: NavPress, 1978).
20. See chapter 3, note 4.
21. See chapter 11, note 9.

Chapter Twelve

HOW TO DEVELOP BIBLICAL CONVICTIONS

———————— ❧ ————————

W hy do we believe as we do? How can we know our convictions are based on the Bible, and be consistent in our convictions? Should we develop convictions only on "doctrine," or should convictions include lifestyle, marriage, child-raising, ministry techniques and methods, and other "nondoctrinal" areas of life?

In many churches and Christian organizations, convictions about proper conduct and methodology are regarded as being just as important as biblical doctrine. Those who belong to these groups subscribe in some fashion to these same convictions. In this way, the convictions (and even doctrines) that many people hold develop not from their personal study but from family background, culture, and the spiritual environment in which they were raised.

These matters are emotional issues to most of us, but we must examine the convictions we now hold, and work to develop true biblical convictions.

Personal convictions are important. A person without them lacks foundations for his life and actions. He becomes unstable, and loses the respect of others.

By learning principles for developing convictions based on the Bible, we can then develop convictions in the gray areas of ethics and honesty about which the Bible does not speak specifically. But first we must distinguish between prejudice and conviction. Many of our dearly treasured convictions are simply prejudices from our backgrounds. Our prejudices are opinions not necessarily founded on fact, but more likely on emotional attachment.

Prejudice is defined as "preconceived judgment or opinion; an opinion or leaning adverse to anything without just grounds or before sufficient knowledge."[1]

We see prejudice every day. Recently my wife, Mary, went to the bank to transfer the title of a trailer we had bought. At the bank she met the man who sold the trailer to us. He ran a pig farm and came dressed in overalls and work shirt. He was heavyset and stuttered when he spoke. As they sat in front of the desk of the young woman notary, Mary watched her as he signed the title. The lady visibly expressed disdain and contempt for him. Her prejudice was obvious.

Prejudice appears in the way we do things. "We've always done it this way" shows the strength of prejudice. Even against demonstrated facts, prejudice causes one to hold to his methods and opinions.

When you make a decision, evaluate whether it is based on conviction that has been thought through and studied, or simply prejudice. Someone has said, "The difference between a conviction and a prejudice is that you can explain a conviction without getting angry."[2] Learn to develop your convictions and suppress prejudice.

In Christian circles, we see conviction in many areas, such as doctrine, the prohibition of certain activities, and methods of operating a church. In most cases we call these "biblical" convictions, but are they? Consider the diagram in figure 12.1. We study the Bible to learn doctrine, which is the foundation for our belief. Every Christian needs this vital foundation. In Scripture we also see certain direct commands—love your neighbor, trust in God, do not commit adultery—which are to be obeyed. But there are many areas of life that are not directly affected by doctrine or commands. Then we must discover biblical principles or patterns such as those regarding worship, giving, evangelism, and discipling. From these principles we make application to follow certain methods and standards of conduct.

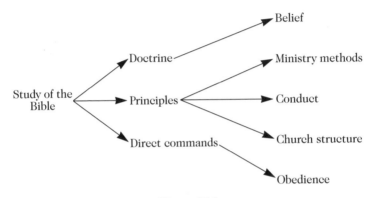

Figure 12.1
The Bible as the Source of Convictions

We must also remember one key fact—*we are twice removed from the Scriptures* when we make applications to our lives from biblical principles. To discern these principles we must make certain assumptions or generalizations about what the Bible says. This removes us one step. Then we make specific application of the principles, the second step. Frequently at this point we become dogmatic and even insist that this particular application is *the* right way to function—for everyone. It may be, but we must remember that we have thus moved from direct Bible teaching to principle to application.

As you can see, great danger exists in attempting to apply such applications to all believers everywhere. So as you develop personal convictions, do all you can to discern between convictions that are directly Bible-based, and those that are once- or twice-removed from Bible teaching. All are valid. God's Spirit does show us patterns of living to follow from the Scripture that are not directly commanded there.

Then, of course, we must also learn to recognize opinions and beliefs based neither on Bible principles nor direct biblical commands, but totally on prejudice. We must not confuse them with biblical convictions, but simply call them our preferences.

Why should we develop personal convictions? In discussing whether it was right to eat certain doubtful foods or to regard a particular day as sacred, Paul said, "Let each man be fully convinced in his own mind" (Romans 14:5). He also warned about being "tossed here and there by waves, and carried about by every wind of doctrine, by the trickery of men" (Ephesians 4:14). Many false doctrines begin by emphasizing issues not clearly taught in Scripture. We need to know what we believe, but we also need to know which issues of conduct are clearly taught in the Bible, and which are matters of conscience or personal choice and leading from God.

Developing personal convictions is important to a stable walk with Christ. By making decisions about certain areas of conduct we do not need to rethink and pray again about the issue on every encounter. To do so would be to spend excessive emotional energy on the wrong issues. Our convictions should set certain guidelines for us *before* we become engrossed and swayed by the emotion of the issue immediately confronting us.

Remember also that convictions are not always permanent. New facts and new teaching — especially new light from God's Word — may cause you to reexamine your thinking. Guard against being closed to change, yet be convinced of where you stand now.

SOURCES OF CONVICTION

Conviction develops from many sources. The first step in making biblical convictions comes when we identify the source of our feelings about an issue. None of these feelings are illegitimate, and they may well be biblical. But we want to make sure the Bible forms the basis of our convictions, rather than relying on our feelings.

BACKGROUND

Much of what we believe and practice comes from our family background and culture. In many years of helping and counseling students and young people, I have often been puzzled by some of their personality characteristics and prejudices. Then I would meet their parents, and I would understand the idiosyncrasies of the student. The similarity was amazing between the parents' speech, mannerisms, attitudes, actions, and appearance, and those of their children.

The geographical location in which we grew up, our social status, and our social heritage—all lay a foundation for our convictions and prejudices that influence us for a lifetime. Because these are so integrated in our lives, they are difficult to identify and doubly difficult to compare with Scripture. Developing biblical convictions involves comparing Bible teaching with these convictions from our backgrounds. Some will change. Many will remain. All must be tested.

EXPERIENCE

A burned finger on a hot stove teaches a child not to touch hot stoves. An autocratic and abusive father often teaches a child to be that kind of mate. Experience builds a multitude of convictions and prejudices even when we don't consciously learn from it. Experience *is* a good teacher—but is not always right.

Our experiences are so personal that generalizations are

impossible. Yet all of us depend on our experiences far more than we would like to admit. You may know someone who insists that Fords are the best automobile made and that he wouldn't buy any other kind, and know someone else who has the same conviction about Chevrolets. Both operate from personal experience—real facts in their lives. And we do the same—in the way we teach our children certain things, the way we treat colds and minor illnesses, the way we talk to certain kinds of people, and in many other things.

Teaching

At home, in school, and in church we have been taught to do and believe certain things and to act in particular ways. Even when we express our own conviction about spiritual beliefs and actions, we can see the effect of what we were taught. In many cases this is good. No one has the time and ability to research all facets of belief and conduct, so we depend on honest and reliable teachers to help us lay foundations in our lives. Sound teaching has a scriptural base and is one of the key functions of the church and home.

A new believer in Christ especially needs teaching, since he must establish a new value system for beliefs and conduct. The teacher and the material are critical. But even with the best teaching we must always search God's Word for ourselves. One whose convictions come only from teaching (especially teaching from only one teacher or source) becomes narrow and dogmatic, unable to explain or defend his convictions from personal knowledge of Scripture. Luke recognized this when he commended the Jews in Berea as being "more noble-minded than those in Thessalonica, for they received the Word with great eagerness, examining the Scriptures daily, to see whether these things were so" (Acts 17:11).

Conduct in the gray areas of Christian living often fits the action of the group rather than carefully considered convictions. Such conformity can be helpful if actions are right.

But rebellion may ensue later when a person realizes these "convictions" may have been ill-founded and were simply preference or prejudice. Teaching can be crucial, but to avoid personal investigation of Scripture is disastrous.

PEER PRESSURE

"Bad company corrupts good morals," Paul told the Corinthians (1 Corinthians 15:33). We become like the people with whom we associate. No matter how proud and independent we may try to be, we soon develop the speech, habits, attitudes, and actions of the group. We also find ourselves adopting their convictions.

The influence of healthy relationships with more mature believers, on the other hand, can be a rich catalyst for the growth of a new believer. Young Christians must be involved in the fellowship of a church or a group of more mature Christians. This positive peer pressure can aid us until we develop our own convictions and lifestyle, because it provides a restraint against sin.

However, unchecked peer pressure from nonChristians can ruin a Christian's spiritual life. The pressure of friends and business associates to do questionable things can be almost unbearable. We must not dissociate from nonChristians, but we must recognize and combat the pressure from them.

ADOPTED CONVICTIONS

As we grow and develop in our faith we find certain people to whom we are greatly attracted because of the quality of their spiritual lives. They may be our teachers or leaders, or business associates and other peers. We observe them. We listen to them. We copy their actions. And finally we adopt their convictions. We become their personal disciple—as Timothy was to Paul. Generally, this does not happen by design on the part of either. It simply happens in the context of life. If this does happen by design, we refer to it as disciple-making—certainly a biblical process greatly needed in the church today.

The father-son, Paul-Timothy relationship teaches convictions in the most powerful way known to Christianity. In deliberate personal discipling of others, we may try to push people to develop personal convictions from Scripture. But we still extensively influence them to conform to our own convictions. Since we know our convictions are being adopted by others, we should have more incentive to be sure our example and teaching come directly from Scripture.

Also, many prominent Christians exert greater influence than we can measure. People adopt the publicly stated convictions and beliefs of well-known leaders. This can be a good influence.

In areas of theology that I have not thoroughly researched and developed, I have adopted the convictions of persons who have proven themselves reliable in other areas of theology and practice that I have researched. Every believer cannot fully develop a full biblical background on every issue. This is a key reason for having pastor-teachers in our churches, and shows how important it is for them to be competent Bible teachers.

Paul instructed the Philippians, "The things you have learned and received and heard and seen *in me*, practice these things" (Philippians 4:9, emphasis added). Previously he had said, "Brethren, join in following my example, and observe those who walk according to the pattern you have in us" (3:17). Paul intended that they adopt his convictions.

But in Acts 17:11 we see the importance of comparing all teaching with Scripture. Surround yourself with good teaching, rather than reading and listening to every available opinion. Then compare all you read and hear to God's Word. If Scripture is silent, use great caution in adopting the convictions of others. Remember that we are told, "Do not believe every spirit, but test the spirits to see whether they are from God; because many false prophets have gone out into the world" (1 John 4:1).

Adopt the convictions of others only with caution and discernment.

The Bible and Conscience

Background, experience, teaching, peer pressure, and adopted convictions must all be confirmed, modified, or done away with as we examine the Bible and allow God to direct us through our conscience. The final court of appeal is Scripture and conscience.

Truly biblical convictions develop from studying the Scripture and praying over specific applications to our lives, and from the personal leading of the Holy Spirit through the conscience. Strive for this kind of conviction. It will stand the test of time and trial. All other convictions will succumb to the challenges of real life.

AREAS AND LEVELS OF CONVICTION

To require a conviction for every act of life would discourage us from developing any convictions at all. Convictions on how to hold a teacup, the precise arrangement of silverware on the table, what kind of gasoline or soap to buy, or whether a tie should be worn to church fall far to the bottom of the list of necessary convictions. We do not want to waste time worrying about convictions that really don't matter.

As we deal with more important areas, we must first define *conviction*. A conviction is a personal belief upon which certain actions are based. It is the motivation or reason behind the action. It is also defined as "a strong persuasion or belief."[3] Also, a conviction must have a base—convictions do not emerge fully formed.

Doctrinal Belief

The foundation for biblical conviction lies in our belief of the Bible's teaching about God, man, sin, Jesus Christ, and salvation. Basic knowledge of Bible teaching or doctrine leads us to certain beliefs or convictions. Doctrinal convictions thus should be formed from the basic Bible truths that are the foundation of the believer's faith. Doctrinal convictions have frequently split churches and denominations, but at the same time they have forced people to carefully consider what they believe.

Doctrinal convictions are important. As a minimum you should know what you believe on:

- the deity of Jesus Christ;
- the authority and inspiration of Scripture;
- salvation;
- the Holy Spirit; and
- the church.

In forming these convictions, study the Bible more than publications about denominational beliefs. Take time to personally examine the Scripture rather than just adopting someone else's beliefs. Your conclusion may be the same as that of your denominational literature, but it will have the foundation of Scripture.

Universal Convictions

Certain actions are universally right or universally wrong. Direct biblical commands and truths apply to all believers everywhere. These should be taught to all and developed as their convictions. For example, all Christians should pray. That statement is universally true, although how and when we pray will vary. It should be a universal conviction.

The only authority to enforce such convictions comes from the Bible. Universal convictions must be based truly in Scripture—rather than being a biased or stretched interpretation of Scripture or tradition. These convictions develop slowly and last for a lifetime.

Write down several things you believe that should be universal convictions. Only a few areas actually fall into this category. We frequently get into conflict when we do not discern between personal convictions and what should be universal convictions.

PERSONAL CONVICTIONS

Some convictions grow out of our personal study of Scripture, and form the basis for much of our personal lifestyle. Although we may desire others to adopt these same convictions, they do not have the strength of convictions based on direct, universal Bible commands. For instance, I may develop the conviction that I should pray with eyes closed and head bowed. This is a personal practice that helps me. I may encourage others to do the same, but I cannot demand that they do it.

Much of our daily activity should fall under the control of personal convictions. We should live not by default, but by purpose. We need to understand the basis for our actions and decisions, yet be open to new information and teaching. Personal convictions can become intolerance and prejudice unless they are regularly examined. We must appeal to the leading of the Holy Spirit and conscience, in conjunction with scriptural principles, in developing personal convictions.

THE PROCESS OF DEVELOPING
PERSONAL BIBLICAL CONVICTIONS

Developing convictions is not an event but a process. It is a step-by-step unfolding—a *developing* process that leads to a conclusion.

It should also be *personal*—with each person studying and thinking to make the conviction personalized, rather than adopted.

Developing convictions should also be *biblical*—having the Bible as the starting point. Scripture differentiates conviction from prejudice and emotional experience. A biblical foundation allows the Holy Spirit and conscience to use the convictions.

No step-by-step method will ever be perfect. However, the following process will give a good basis for logically and honestly developing personal convictions. As you follow these guidelines, God will have the opportunity to lead you and influence your thinking and convictions.

THE BASICS OF THE CHRISTIAN LIFE

Many believers become concerned with the fringe elements of the life of faith before dealing with basic issues. Jesus said to "seek first His kingdom" (Matthew 6:33). God wants us to operate on a priority system. He wants us to do certain things first. We should not jump to step three before doing step one.

The most foundational issue is personal salvation—knowing that we have personally received Christ as Savior, thereby becoming a Christian. This step requires a personal, life-changing decision to receive the forgiveness of sin that Christ offers (read John 1:12, 3:16; Romans 3:23; 2 Corinthians 5:17).

After becoming a Christian, other basics are needed for growth to maturity. These elements of the Christian life provide a basis on which to build personal convictions.

1. *Have a daily devotional time with God.* Set aside a time that includes regular reading of the Bible and meditation on what you read. Also include a time of prayer for yourself and others.[4]

2. *Obey what you know*. God convicts us of many things He wants us to do before giving insight into other areas. Perhaps there is an area of your life, specific attitudes or activities, that you know God wants changed. Obey Him in these areas first. God will then give you additional insight and leading.

3. *Have fellowship with other Christians*. The biblical view of the body of Christ shows that Christians need one another. Seek fellowship in a church and with individual believers in small groups. "Encourage one another day after day, as long as it is still called 'Today'" (Hebrews 3:13). "And let us consider how to stimulate one another to love and good deeds, not forsaking our own assembling together, as is the habit of some, but encouraging one another; and all the more, as you see the day drawing near" (10:24-25). We need the influence of the body of Christ on our lives.

4. *Make Christ the center of your life*. Many people become Christians, but hold back certain areas of their lives from God's control. Even though at the time of salvation they really intended to make Christ the Lord of their lives, in reality they have not done so. Your spiritual growth may be stifled if Christ is not your Lord. This is a decision of the will. Simply pray and tell Christ you want Him to be the Lord of your life as well as your Savior. Name the specific areas that you have withheld from Him and ask for His direction in turning them over to Him. Make a clear and specific decision to live as Christ's disciple.

5. *Confess known sin*. "If I regard wickedness in my heart, the Lord will not hear" (Psalm 66:18). "If we confess our sins, He is faithful and righteous to forgive us our sins and to cleanse us from all

unrighteousness" (1 John 1:9). Unconfessed sin hinders our relationship with God and prevents growth. Clear your communication channels with God by confessing sins you know are present in your life.

These are the basics—the "musts" of the Christian life.

Further Steps in Developing Personal Convictions

Other decisions to make in developing personal convictions include *accepting what the Bible teaches about honesty and morality*. Personal convictions should grow out of principles based on the clear teaching of the Bible. Once you understand and agree with basic biblical teaching on lying, cheating, stealing, sexual morality, and other aspects of ethics and honesty, you have the basis from which to establish principles and make specific applications to your life.

Identify the specific area of concern. Write out the particular problem or area for which you wish to develop a conviction or make a decision. For instance, you may be concerned about honest representation of a product you sell. Write out the specific questions in your mind. "I know my product has certain limitations. Should I volunteer the information to the customer or wait until asked? My boss says to wait, but I am unsure of the ethics of the situation." From this you can identify the specific issue: It is a matter of honest representation.

You may also want to detail other facts of the situation to clarify it in your mind.

Search out related biblical instructions. After identifying the issue, research and record specific Bible passages that may apply. Look for similar incidents or illustrations in both Old and New Testaments. Use a concordance to locate additional verses. List each verse or passage down the left side of a page, and then put a six- or seven-word summary of the verse by each reference. A *Nave's Topical Bible*[5] is an excellent aid in this kind of study.

Pray. As you read the various passages, pray that God will give you direction. Pray about your specific need. Ask God to guide you to the right convictions. The combination of Scripture and the Holy Spirit working in your mind and conscience will give you the needed direction. Write down some of your thoughts and impressions as you pray.

Ask key questions. As you pray, consider your response to several questions relating to the result of your decision or conviction. Oklahoma businessman Gene Warr created this list to help people make decisions in questionable matters.

1. Does the Bible say it is wrong? (1 Samuel 15:22, John 14:21)
2. Will it hurt my body? (1 Corinthians 6:19-20)
3. Will it hurt my mind? (Philippians 4:8)
4. Will it enslave me? (1 Corinthians 6:12)
5. Is it good stewardship? (1 Corinthians 4:2)
6. Will it glorify God? (1 Corinthians 10:31, Philippians 1:20)
7. Will it profit and edify others? (1 Corinthians 10:33, Hebrews 10:24)
8. Will it help me to serve? (1 Corinthians 9:19, 10:23-24)
9. Is it worth imitating? (1 Corinthians 11:1, Philippians 4:9)
10. Will it cause others to stumble? (Romans 14:21, 1 Corinthians 8:9)
11. Is it the best? (Philippians 1:9-10)

Seek counsel. At this point, after you have done sufficient study and thinking on your own to form a background for the suggestions of others, seek counsel from someone whose life you respect and who looks to Scripture in his own decisions. You may already know the direction God is leading you, and this counsel will be primarily for confirmation. Ask this person to evaluate the conclusions you have reached.

One word of caution is needed: I have had people come to me for counsel who really did not want counsel—they wanted me to agree with their decision and soothe their conscience. This usually happens when a person wants badly to do something and ignores his conscience, deciding to fulfill his own desire.

Make a decision. By this time you should know the direction God wants you to take or the convictions on which you are to act. Take a step of faith and act on the conviction. As you do, listen to your conscience.

As you formulate your conviction, try to discern its extent and definiteness. If you intend it to be a lifetime conviction, be certain of your foundation. Other convictions might be appropriate for a few months or a year. In other cases you may have a tentative conviction, not yet tried and proven.

Evaluate the results. As you begin acting on the basis of your conviction, evaluate the response of your conscience. If you have continued peace and your conscience is sensitive to God, you can be assured of being in God's will. If you experience lack of peace and pangs of conscience you need to review the process again and rethink your conviction.

Form habits. One result of developing convictions is forming habits that reflect these convictions. We should want to act on the basis of conviction, with these actions becoming ingrained in our lives. For example, if we develop a conviction to have a regular devotional time with God, we can build a habit of setting aside time each morning to do so. Building these habits means we do not have to constantly redevelop our convictions.

Habit is one of the most powerful friends we can have,

as well as our most potent enemy when our habits are wrong. Since so much of life flows from habit, special attention needs to be given to building godly habits based on biblical convictions.

SUMMARY

Personal convictions do not develop in a matter of days or months, but over a period of years and through careful prayer and study. But we are impatient people, unwilling to go through the process of developing conviction in a step-by-step manner. We want instant maturity, not slow growth. Growth that takes time and effort, however, lasts for a lifetime.

As you think of areas in your life where convictions are needed, you may wonder what to work on first. Think of these three stages of development:

1. As a *new Christian* or one who has not grown spiritually, concentrate on developing convictions in the basics of the Christian life. These would include your daily time in the Word and prayer, Bible study, basic areas of obedience, the lordship of Jesus Christ, marriage and family relationships, and witnessing. In other areas you will at this point most likely adopt many of the convictions of your church or Christian friends.
2. As a *young, growing Christian* who has developed some basic convictions, you need to develop further convictions in the basic beliefs and doctrines of the Christian life. Personal Bible study is a must in this phase of growth. Form basic convictions on the doctrines of salvation, the inspiration of Scripture, evangelism and disciple-making, the church, the Holy Spirit, and Christian character (such

qualities as love, peace, and patience). Begin to develop your personal skills and gifts in outward ministry.

3. As a *mature Christian*, develop convictions one at a time in the areas of ministry, social issues, personal ethics and conduct, and lifestyle.

Obviously, at any point of growth, issues that demand decisions force you to study and develop convictions as they arise. In each of these phases of growth, avoid being sidetracked into unimportant issues and debates. Keep your focus on the basic personal issues of spiritual growth and ministry.

As you reflect on the content of this book, ask God to lead you into personal, *biblically based* convictions. Know what the Bible teaches and build your life on that. Train your conscience to guide you in the gray areas of conduct. Pray that your life will always reflect a deep sensitivity to the Holy Spirit in every area of conduct. There is no substitute for the serenity and certainty that comes from a life of conviction, springing from daily quiet times with God and from a deep personal study of His Word. Only then can we walk in the quiet assurance that God is in control of our lives.

Notes
1. *Webster's New Collegiate Dictionary*, p. 907.
2. *Bits and Pieces*, November 1973, p. 6.
3. *Webster's New Collegiate Dictionary*, p. 249.
4. See chapter 3, note 6.
5. Orville J. Nave, *Nave's Topical Bible* (Chicago: Moody).

A Bible Study on Honesty, Morality, and Conscience

———————————— ∾ ————————————

Contents

BEFORE YOU BEGIN

⟋⟍

Living a life of integrity before God and before our fellow human beings is clearly a scriptural goal for Christians—and one that takes continual commitment and learning. It is not enough to have someone else tell us how to do it, even if they could tell us everything. True biblical convictions come only through our own searching.

This Bible study helps you do just that—to search, to study, and to build biblical conviction. Designed to supplement and personalize the contents of this book, this twelve-lesson Bible study can be used in different ways:

Individual study. For your individual benefit, you can complete each lesson of the study as you read through the corresponding chapter.

Small groups. Perhaps the best use of the course is in a weekly discussion group of six to ten people, studying one lesson each week. Each group member should answer the study questions for that week's lesson before the group meets, and the group leader should both answer the questions and prepare for the group meeting by studying the "Guidelines for Group Discussion" in each lesson.

Classes. Larger groups and more formal classes can also complete the course profitably. Again, it is important that each individual complete the study questions before the class meets.

The lessons in this study correspond to the twelve chapters of this book. Each one has from five to twelve study questions for you to answer in the spaces provided. Many of the questions will help you apply to your life the biblical truths you are studying. Each lesson also has the following parts:

■ *Guidelines for group discussion.* This includes questions and ideas to help the leader stimulate group interaction. The leader should also formulate his or her own questions and ideas, which are appropriate for the group.

■ *Suggested Scripture memory.* It will take work to memorize the verses and to review them often enough to keep them word perfect in your memory. But knowing and meditating on them will help impress in your life the lessons you are learning. Reviewing the verses with each other weekly when the group meets will encourage you in your memorization.

■ *Special project.* You will especially enjoy these interesting assignments on each topic, which you will do in the week following your discussion on that topic.

You may find in your group discussion that you want to spend more than one week on some lessons. For example, a group including high school or college students may want to spend two weeks on lesson 8, "Honesty as a Student"; or a group including mostly parents may want to spend extra time on lesson 7, "Honesty in the Home."

The Holy Spirit will guide you as you study and seek to apply Scripture. And as you listen to others in your group, you will benefit greatly from the insights God has revealed to them.

God will bless you as you study. Follow the example of the Bereans, who "received the word with great eagerness, examining the Scriptures daily, to see whether these things were so" (Acts 17:11, NASB).

Lesson 1
THE DILEMMAS OF HONESTY OR THE PROBLEM DEFINED

1. Read chapter 1 of *Honesty, Morality, and Conscience*. List two or three questions about honesty that you have encountered and for which you would like to find answers.

2. Examine Psalm 15.

   a. List the ways honesty is demonstrated in the psalmist's life and the forms of dishonesty he avoids.

   b. What does this passage indicate about the importance of honesty to our relationship with God?

3. Read 1 Samuel 15:1-29.

   a. What did Saul do that specifically displeased God?

   b. What was God's response to Saul's action?

   c. What do you learn about God's character in verse 29?

4. What evidences can you list from the world around you that confirm or deny Joan Beck's statement on page 14 that "lying is commonplace in our society"?

5. Write in your own words the guideline Paul gave in 2 Corinthians 8:21.

The purpose of this session is for you to share and discuss personal feelings and needs in the area of honesty. Although free discussion is encouraged, be sure to center at least half of your time on the Scripture references given in the study questions. The questions and suggestions that follow are for the group leader to use in guiding the discussion.

1. Talk about question 1. (Write several of the questions on index cards for reference in future studies.)

2. Share your answers to both parts of question 2. (Discuss any words or concepts in the passage that you have questions about.) Which of the standards of honesty listed in Psalm 15 are the most difficult to attain in today's world?

3. Discuss your study of 1 Samuel 15:1-29 (question 3). Can you identify personally with the way Saul acted? What do you think is the most important lesson for us from this incident?

4. Pick one of the case studies on pages 10-11 and discuss what you would do in that situation.

5. Compile a list of specific areas of life in which honesty is most difficult for you (for example, business dealings, speech, or obeying traffic laws).

6. Share your answers to question 5.

7. Discuss the Scripture memory verse and the special project for the coming week.

8. Close your time in group prayer.

Suggested Scripture Memory: Psalm 15:1-2

Special Project: In the coming week, ask five people what specific kinds of dishonesty bother them the most, either in their own lives or in the world around them. Jot down some of their answers so you can talk about them in the discussion group next week.

Lesson 2
YOUR CONSCIENCE — FRIEND OR FOE?

1. Read chapter 2 of *Honesty, Morality, and Conscience*. From your reading, record any questions you have about the conscience.

2. Look up and record the dictionary definition of *conscience*.

3. Describe an instance from your life when your conscience troubled you. How did you respond to it?

4. List the four basic means God uses to direct us (see pages 22-25). Which are the most important? Explain.

5. Look up 2 Corinthians 1:12 in as many translations as you can. What did the consciences of Paul and Timothy communicate about their way of life?

6. Study Romans 2:14-15 and 9:1. What does the conscience "bear witness" of?

7. Look up the following passages: Acts 24:16, 2 Corinthians 4:2, 1 Timothy 1:18-19, Hebrews 13:18. Write a brief sentence on what you learn about the conscience from each one and what evidence you see that the conscience passes moral judgment.

8. Is anything troubling your conscience now? Either here or on a separate piece of paper describe it, and write out several things you could do to bring peace to your conscience.

The purpose of this discussion is to help each of you understand the meaning of conscience as it is used in Scripture and how God can and will use your conscience to help you make right decisions.

1. A good way to start each session is to review the previous week's memory verse. Take a few minutes to break into pairs for review of Psalm 15:1-2.

2. Discuss last week's special project. What issues of dishonesty are people troubled by?

3. What is an important thing you learned in preparing the study this week or in reading the assigned chapter?

4. Review the definition of *conscience* (question 2). How does this definition relate to what you learned about the conscience in Scripture? (You may also want to examine the definition of conscience given in a Bible dictionary or encyclopedia.)

5. Discuss the four major ways God directs us (question 4). Which are the most important? How do they relate to each other?

6. Discuss your answers to question 7. Which of these verses is the most helpful to you in understanding the scriptural view of conscience? What evidence do you see that the conscience passes moral judgment?

7. If the conscience makes a wrong judgment, how will we know it?

8. Read aloud 1 Timothy 1:18-19. What can be the result of ignoring your conscience?

9. Summarize together what you have learned about the conscience from this session. What further questions do you have?

10. Share with each other any specific concerns you may have as a result of this study, and pray together about those.

11. Discuss the Scripture memory verse and the special project for the coming week.

Suggested Scripture Memory: 2 Corinthians 1:12

Special Project: Ask God each day in the coming week to prick your conscience about some issue that day. Make a note of the ways He answers your prayer.

Lesson 3
HOW TO USE AND RESPOND TO YOUR CONSCIENCE

———————— ❧ ————————

1. Read chapter 3 of *Honesty, Morality, and Conscience*. Make a note of one or two strong impressions that come to your mind as you read—either positive or negative. Also record any questions you have.

2. Read Hebrews 9:14. Rewrite this verse in your own words.

3. Read Acts 23:1. Why do you think Paul was able to say this?

4. Study 1 Timothy 1:19, 3:8-9, and Hebrews 10:19-22. How would you describe the relationship between conscience and faith?

5. Read 1 Peter 3:16. What is one result of a good conscience?

6. List the kinds of conscience described in the following verses: 1 Corinthians 8:7,12; Titus 1:15; 1 Timothy 4:1-2.

7. Consider how the teaching in 1 Corinthians 8:9-12 can be applied to your life. What actions of yours could be a stumbling block to others?

8. Consider figure 1 on page 42. What makes the one response to conscience wrong?

9. Examine 1 Corinthians 2:9-16. How does this passage shed light on the difference between the conscience of a Christian and that of a nonChristian?

10. Consider the steps for training and strengthening your conscience listed on pages 43-45. Which step do you need to develop the most? Write down one thing you intend to do this week to help you meet that need.

GUIDELINES FOR GROUP DISCUSSION
The purpose of this session is to deepen your understanding of conscience and to give you practical help in responding to it.
1. Review your memorization of 2 Corinthians 1:12.
2. Discuss last week's special project. In what areas did God speak to you through your conscience?
3. Share an important thing you learned in preparing the study this week or in reading the assigned chapter.
4. Read your paraphrases of Hebrews 9:14 (question 2). What would be the result of a cleansed conscience?
5. Discuss your answers to question 4.
6. How would you define a "good" conscience?
7. Share your answers to question 7. Discuss practical steps you can take to keep from doing things that are a stumbling block to those with a weak conscience.
8. Discuss your answers to question 8. What part does God play in each of the two responses listed in the illustration? Are any steps left out of the illustration? What are some possible problems a person might encounter in each of the steps?
9. Discuss your answers to question 9.
10. Share your answers to question 10, and help each other with ideas for making your applications practical.
11. Summarize together what you have learned about the conscience from this session.
12. Close in group prayer.
13. Discuss the Scripture memory verse and the special project for the coming week.

Suggested Scripture Memory: 1 Timothy 1:5

Special Project: Ask three nonChristians in the coming week how they would define *conscience*. Also ask, "How do you think God relates to your conscience?"

Lesson 4
HONESTY —
THE BIBLICAL MANDATE

---～---

1. Read chapter 4 of *Honesty, Morality, and Conscience*. Make a note of specific questions you have that are not answered directly in the chapter.

2. Look up the dictionary definitions of *honest* and *honesty*.

3. Categorize the following references under the topics of "Speech," "Actions," and "Thoughts": Psalm 51:6; Proverbs 16:13; Luke 6:31; Romans 9:1, 12:17; Philippians 4:8; Colossians 3:9; James 4:17.

4. Examine Psalm 15:3 and 101:5. What is the common issue in these verses?

5. Study the account of Ananias and Sapphira in Acts 5:1-11.

   a. Who were they deceiving?

   b. How could they have avoided death?

   c. What is the connection between being honest with men and being honest with God?

   d. What are some ways you are tempted to practice deceit?

6. Paraphrase Ephesians 4:25,29.

7. Read the Ten Commandments in Exodus 20:1-17. Which of them are related to honesty?

234

8. Tell what each of the following passages teaches about God's standard for truth: John 14:6, 17:17; Colossians 2:8-10; 1 Peter 1:24–2:2.

The purpose of this session is to emphasize the biblical teaching on honesty and to lay a foundation for later studies dealing with specific areas of life.

1. Review your memorization of 1 Timothy 1:5.
2. Discuss last week's project. How did your nonChristian friends define *conscience*? What relationship did they see between God and conscience?
3. Review the definitions of *honest* and *honesty* (question 2).
4. How did you categorize the verses in question 3?
5. Discuss your answers to the four parts of question 5. How would you summarize the lessons we should learn from Acts 5:1-11?
6. Share your answers to question 8, and discuss the meaning of the word *truth*.
7. Discuss why you think people lie and which reasons you believe are the most common.
8. Summarize what you have learned about the Bible's teaching on honesty.
9. Close in group prayer.
10. Discuss the Scripture memory verse and special project for the coming week.

Suggested Scripture Memory: Ephesians 4:25

Special Project: Choose one of the verses from your study so far that has impressed you about the biblical standard for honesty. Meditate on the verse at least once each day in the coming week. Think particularly about how the verse relates to specific circumstances in your life. Write down the major insights you gain.

Lesson 5
THE PROBLEM OF PEER PRESSURE

1. Read chapter 5 of *Honesty, Morality, and Conscience*. Record any questions and observations you have.

2. What pressures to conform affect you most?

3. Write in your own words the basic commands in Romans 12:2.

4. Record the definition of *conformity*.

5. Read Ephesians 4:28, Colossians 3:5-8, and 1 Peter 1:14-15. From these verses, write a statement about the relationship between our life today and our former nonChristian life.

6. How do 1 Peter 2:16 and Galatians 5:13 relate to conformity?

7. Review the list of suggestions on pages 68-69 on how to withstand pressure from others. Which step is the hardest for you, and why?

8. Examine Colossians 3:15 and Hebrews 3:12-13, 10:24-25. What part does Christian fellowship have in countering adverse pressure to conform?

9. From the following verses, make a list of the kinds of conformity that are good: 1 Corinthians 11:1, Ephesians 5:1-2, 2 Thessalonians 3:7-9, Hebrews 13:7, 3 John 11.

10. How does the teaching of Proverbs 13:20 relate to pressure from others?

11. Read Philippians 4:8. How can a Christian guard his mind from worldly conformity?

12. In what specific area are you encountering pressure to conform? What can you do about it? List one thing that you will do this week.

GUIDELINES FOR GROUP DISCUSSION

The purpose of this session is to help you recognize and correct areas of your life where conformity to the world is affecting you.

1. Review your memorization of Ephesians 4:25.
2. Discuss last week's project. What verses did you select, and what insights did you gain in meditating on them?
3. Share an important thing you learned in preparing the study this week or in reading the assigned chapter.
4. Discuss your answers to question 2.
5. Read aloud Romans 12:2, and discuss your answers to question 3. What is the "world" mentioned in this verse? How do we renew our minds?
6. Talk about your answers to question 6.
7. Discuss your answers to question 8. How can you apply these truths to your group?
8. Define *lifestyle*, then discuss your answers to question 9. Is there a "Christian lifestyle"? If so, what is it?
9. Read aloud Romans 8:29 and 2 Corinthians 3:17-18. How does this relate to pressure from the world to conform?
10. Discuss your answers to questions 10 and 11. What practical actions can you take to overcome pressure to conform?
11. Share your responses to question 12. Help each other with ideas for making your applications practical. Close in group prayer.
12. Discuss the memory verse and the special project.

Suggested Scripture Memory: Proverbs 13:20

Special Project: Sometime during the coming week take ten minutes to observe people in a crowd, looking for evidence of how they conform. Do this again at a Christian gathering. Record some of your findings, and examine how these ways of conforming are also present in your life.

Lesson 6
HONESTY AND ETHICS
IN BUSINESS AND WORK

———————— ∽ ————————

1. Read chapter 6 of *Honesty, Morality, and Conscience*.
   Record any questions and observations you have.

2. List any recent instances of dishonesty in business and work
   that you have personally observed.

3. Read Deuteronomy 25:13-16. List several types of business
   dealings to which you think these verses would apply.

4. Study Romans 13:1-3. To what extent should a Christian
   obey the law?

5. How would you relate the following passages of Romans
   12:17-21 and Ephesians 5:11-12 to the question of what
   responsibility a Christian has for confronting dishonesty?

6. What guidelines for honesty with your employer can you
   derive from Ephesians 6:5-9?

7. How do the following passages relate to work? Consider
   Luke 16:10-13 and Colossians 3:23-24.

8. Write out the details of any circumstance involving a question on honesty that concerns you in your work.

GUIDELINES FOR GROUP DISCUSSION
The purpose of this session is to help you apply principles of honesty and ethics to business and work. In your discussion, do not get

sidetracked to theoretical problems that none of you has encountered. Stay with the principal issues as they apply to your lives.

1. Review your memorization of Proverbs 13:20.
2. Review last week's project. What kinds of conformity did you observe?
3. Share an important thing you learned in preparing the lesson this week or in reading the assigned chapter.
4. Discuss each of the five commands of business ethics listed on pages 73-80. Which of the commands do you think is the most difficult to follow? Which do you think is the most important? Explain.
5. Discuss your answers to question 4. How does the teaching in this passage relate specifically to circumstances in your life?
6. Share your answers to question 5.
7. Discuss your answers to question 6. How can these guidelines be implemented?
8. Talk about your answers to question 7. How can you make your work an act of worship to God?
9. Share your responses to question 8. Discuss ideas for applying scriptural principles to the circumstances you listed.
10. Close in group prayer.
11. Discuss the memory verse and the project for the coming week.

Suggested Scripture Memory: Luke 16:10 (Remember to continue reviewing the verses you learned in previous weeks.)

Special Project: At your job this week observe how many people waste the employer's time by arriving late and how many things of questionable ethics you see people do. Check yourself in these same areas.

Lesson 7
HONESTY
IN THE HOME

———————————⟨∿⟩———————————

1. Read chapter 7 of *Honesty, Morality, and Conscience*. Make a note of situations in the book that are similar to situations you have encountered in your family.

2. Read Ephesians 6:1-4, noting the responsibilities of both children and fathers.

   a. How can a father's dishonesty hurt his ability to fulfill his obligations as listed in this passage?

   b. How can a child's dishonesty hurt his ability to obey and honor his or her parents?

3. Read Ephesians 4:29. How can this teaching be applied in your family?

4. Study Ephesians 5:22-24. In what ways is honesty necessary for a wife to fulfill her responsibility to her husband?

5. Study Ephesians 5:25-28. In what ways is honesty necessary for a husband to fulfill his responsibility to his wife?

6. From each of the following passages, tell why parents should use Scripture in training their children: 2 Timothy 3:14-17, Hebrews 4:12-13, 1 Peter 1:24-25.

7. Examine Titus 2:7-8. How can these statements be applied to parents training their children?

8. Examine the causes of dishonesty listed on pages 107-109. Which of these do you think affects your children the most?

9. Beginning on page 109 are several steps for helping children develop honesty. Choose one of them that relates most to your family's needs. What one or two things can you do this week to apply this with your children?

GUIDELINES FOR GROUP DISCUSSION

The purpose of this session is to explore biblical principles for honesty in your family.

1. Review your memorization of Luke 16:10.
2. Discuss last week's project. What things did you observe at your job?
3. Share an important thing you learned in preparing this study this week or in reading the assigned chapter.
4. Share and discuss your answers to questions 2-8. Pay particular attention in your discussion to scriptural standards for relationships and how these standards can be applied in your home.
5. The principles in 1 Corinthians 12 about the unity of Christians are true in a particularly deep away for a Christian family. Read aloud 1 Corinthians 12:26-27, and discuss how this passage relates to your family.
6. Share your responses to question 9. Discuss with each other ideas for improving your applications.
7. Close in group prayer.
8. Discuss the memory verse and the project for the coming week.

Suggested Scripture Memory: Ephesians 6:4

Special Project: If you have children, ask each one to write down his or her definition of *honesty*. Ask your children also if there are things they would like to see changed in your family.

Lesson 8
HONESTY
AS A STUDENT

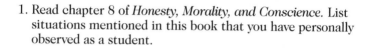

1. Read chapter 8 of *Honesty, Morality, and Conscience*. List situations mentioned in this book that you have personally observed as a student.

2. Read Luke 6:31. List three ways that you would like other students to show respect for you and your schoolwork, keeping in mind that you must respect them in the same way.

3. Record the definitions of *deceit* and *deceive*.

4. Read these verses in Proverbs 11, and summarize how they relate to cheating: 3, 5, 6, 19, 27, and 31.

5. Paraphrase Proverbs 20:17.

6. Study Proverbs 6:6-11 and 24:30-34. How do the principles given in these passages relate to schoolwork?

7. Consider the cheating incident described on pages 119-120. In your opinion, the student should have . . .

   ❑ kept quiet, not worrying about the cheating.
   ❑ waited until after the exam and then spoken to the professor.
   ❑ done exactly what he did.
   ❑ preceded his statement with "I'm a Christian and. . . ."
   ❑ written an anonymous letter about the cheating.
   ❑ observed who was cheating and reported them specifically.

   Explain your choice.

8. Suppose you had to choose between failing and cheating. List some of the results of each choice. For more insight on this question read Proverbs 12:28, 14:12; Matthew 6:33; and Romans 8:38-39.

9. Read Psalm 26:4-5 and 119:104. If you have not already done so, make a commitment to pursue total honesty in your schoolwork and in your profession. State this commitment in your own words.

GUIDELINES FOR GROUP DISCUSSION

The purpose of this session is to help you understand long-term results of both cheating and not cheating, and to make a commitment not to cheat. (If your group has few or no students, you can approach the discussion from the viewpoint of how to help your children cope with cheating or how these same principles relate to nonacademic areas.)

1. Review your memorization of Ephesians 6:4.
2. Discuss last week's project. What comments did your children make?
3. Share an important thing you learned in preparing your lesson this week or in reading the assigned chapter.
4. Talk about your answers to questions 2-8.
5. Do you think failure can actually be good? How?
6. Discuss the implications of the requested commitment in question 9. Close in group prayer, jointly reaffirming your intention to meet God's standard in this area.
7. Discuss the memory verse and the project for the coming week.

Suggested Scripture Memory: Proverbs 20:17

Special Project: Ask a schoolteacher to describe to you how his or her students cheat or try to cheat, and ask for the teacher's opinion as to why students cheat. Ask your children or other children the same questions.

Lesson 9
HONESTY
IN THE CHURCH

1. Read chapter 9 of *Honesty, Morality, and Conscience*. From your reading, record observations you have of your own church.

2. Summarize what each of the following verses teaches about relationships among Christians and why honesty is important in each of the aspects you mention: Romans 12:9-10, 15:1; Ephesians 4:32; 1 Peter 1:22; 1 John 3:16-18.

3. Describe the proper characteristics of a Christian's speech as they are given in Ephesians 5:3-4.

4. Study Philippians 2:3-4. How should these verses apply to the way you communicate with others?

5. a. Why are the concepts of Matthew 5:23-24 and 18:15 important in resolving conflict?

   b. Record an instance when the principles in these verses have been applied in your relationship with someone, either by yourself or by the other person. What was the result?

6. After examining the following verses, write a statement about how a person can become more teachable: Proverbs 12:15, 13:20, and 15:31-32.

7. After considering the above questions, is there someone with whom you need to improve your relationship? How can you improve?

8. Read 1 Timothy 3:2-13. Pick two of the leadership characteristics listed there, and describe specifically how you would recognize these in a potential Christian leader.

9. Review 1 Timothy 3:6. What can happen when an immature Christian is placed in a position of church leadership?

The purpose of this session is to help you examine how you relate to others in your church and to understand qualifications for church leadership.
1. Review your memorization of Proverbs 20:17.
2. Discuss last week's project. What things did you learn from the schoolteacher or from children?
3. Share an important thing you learned in preparing the study or in reading the chapter.
4. Discuss your answers to questions 2-6, paying particular attention in your discussion to biblical standards for Christian relationships.
5. Describe how you should express criticism or disagreement to others.
6. Do you think conflict in relationships among Christians is unavoidable?
7. Discuss you answers to questions 7 and 8.
8. What do you think are the most important qualifications for church leadership?
9. Talk about your responses to question 9. Discuss problems you have observed in your church, and examine how honest communication and mature leadership can solve these problems.
10. Close in group prayer.
11. Discuss the memory verses and the project for the coming week.

Suggested Scripture Memory: Romans 12:9-10

Special Project: Study the levels of communication listed on pages 138-139. Pick a relationship that is important to you, but that is still at level 4 or 5 in your communication. Work and plan specifically to move to level 2.

Lesson 10
HONESTY WITH YOURSELF

————————— ⌇ —————————

1. Read chapter 10 of *Honesty, Morality, and Conscience*. Record any observations and questions you have.

2. Look back at the definitions you recorded for *deceit* and *deceive* in lesson 8, and summarize them here.

3. From James 1:22-24, describe the relationship between disobeying the Scripture and self-deception.

4. Paraphrase Romans 12:3.

5. Examine 1 Corinthians 3:18. According to this passage, how and why should we avoid self-deception?

6. Read 1 Corinthians 12:12-22, and summarize its teaching as it relates to self-image.

7. Study Galatians 6:1-5. What principles about self-image should be kept in mind . . .

   a. when dealing with someone who has sinned?

   b. when helping others with their needs and problems?

8. Begin a list of what you consider your strengths and abilities and another of your weaknesses and needs.

GUIDELINES FOR GROUP DISCUSSION
The purpose of this session is to help you have a realistic and honest view of yourself.

1. Review your memorization of Romans 12:9-10.
2. Discuss last week's project. Did you see any improvements in your relationship?
3. Share an important thing you learned about yourself in preparing the lesson this week or in reading the assigned chapter.
4. Discuss your answers to questions 2-7.
5. What is the right balance between the extremes of an inferior self-image and false pride?
6. How can we be dishonest with God?
7. What is the right response to being disappointed about our physical features?
8. Write down on an index card one area in which you have a poor self-image and want to change. Don't sign your name. The group leader should collect the cards and redistribute them to the group members at random. Try to identify who wrote the card you were given. Most of you will probably have a difficult time in identification. The closer and smaller your group, the easier it will be.
9. Discuss what you see as the major strengths of each person in your group.
10. Share your work on question 8, and discuss the special project.
11. Close in group prayer.
12. Discuss the memory verse.

Suggested Scripture Memory: Romans 12:3

Special Project: Review the eight steps for self-evaluation on pages 169-170, and follow them this week, using your work in question 8 as a beginning.

Lesson 11
SEXUAL MORALITY

—————————————~⌐/~—————————————

1. Read chapter 11 of *Honesty, Morality, and Conscience*. Record any observations and questions you have as you read.

2. Summarize the teaching of each of these verses: 1 Corinthians 6:18, 1 Thessalonians 4:3, 1 Peter 2:11.

3. Study Ephesians 5:23-33 and Hebrews 13:4. How do you think having a biblical view of marriage can be a deterrent to premarital and extramarital sex?

4. Read Matthew 5:28, 2 Corinthians 10:5, and Colossians 3:2. How and why should a Christian guard his thoughts?

5. How do you think Matthew 6:22-23 applies to the issue of pornography?

6. Explain how each of the following passages applies to masturbation: 1 Corinthians 6:18-20, Galatians 5:16-19, 1 Thessalonians 4:3-7.

7. Read Exodus 20:14,17. What is the difference between the commandments not to commit adultery and not to covet your neighbor's wife?

8. Read Matthew 5:8, 1 Corinthians 3:16-17, 2 Corinthians 7:1, and 1 Thessalonians 4:7. Choose the verse that is most helpful in challenging you to moral purity, and write it out. (Or select a verse other than those listed.) Tell why you chose the verse you did.

9. Is there a specific action you should take toward sexual purity and personal holiness? Either here or on a separate piece of paper, plan this step of action.

GUIDELINES FOR GROUP DISCUSSION

The purpose of this session is to challenge you to a life of sexual purity and personal holiness. (You may prefer to divide the group between men and women for all or part of this session's discussion.)

1. Review your memorization of Romans 12:3.
2. Discuss last week's project. What conclusions do you have from your self-evaluation?
3. Share an important thing you learned in preparing the study or in reading the chapter.
4. Talk about your answers to questions 2-8.
5. Discuss the issues mentioned in chapter 11 that are the most relevant to your group, emphasizing especially how biblical standards relate to the issues.
6. Discuss the memory verse and the project for the coming week.
7. Close in group prayer.

Suggested Scripture Memory: Memorize the verse you selected in question 8.

Special Project: Prepare a small chart on an index card with a blank square for each hour you will be awake during a three-day period in the coming week. Learn the memory verse you selected, and plan to meditate on it once each hour during the three-day period. Keep the card with you, and place a check in the square for each hour during which you thought about the verse at least briefly. You will probably miss some hours, but do your best. Make a note of new insights you gain about the verse. After the three days, you'll be surprised how often the verse will again come to mind.

Lesson 12
HOW TO DEVELOP BIBLICAL CONVICTIONS

———————————— ∿ ————————————

1. Read chapter 12 of *Honesty, Morality, and Conscience*. Make a note of any observations or questions you have.

2. From the following verses, explain why you should develop personal convictions: Romans 14:22-23, Ephesians 4:14, Colossians 2:6-8, 1 Thessalonians 1:5, Hebrews 4:12.

3. Read John 9:13-38. What factors led to the blind man's belief in Christ? Why do you think the Pharisees did not believe?

4. Read Acts 17:10-12. On what basis did these Berean Jews believe in Christ?

5. Read Paul's statement of one of his convictions in Romans 8:38-39. How should a conviction like this affect a believer's life?

6. Read another of Paul's convictions in Romans 14:14. How did this affect Paul's thinking and actions? (See verses 13-17 also.)

7. Choose three of the following areas (or others you think of), and write a statement summarizing your convictions in each area: devotional time with God, fellowship with believers, Scripture as the authority for your beliefs and conduct, prayer, witnessing, giving to others, personal time with your family, honesty in speech, moral purity, and helping others grow spiritually.

8. Look back through the eleven previous lessons. Record at least one major lesson you have learned. In what ways has your life been changed? Are there other areas in which you now need to develop more convictions?

9. Choose an area from question 7 or 8 in which you desire to develop greater conviction. List at least three things you could do in the next two months to develop that conviction. Refer to the guidelines on pages 217-223.

GUIDELINES FOR GROUP DISCUSSION

The purpose of this session is to help you develop personal convictions.

1. Review the verse you chose to memorize last week, and share insights you gained in meditating on the verse.
2. Share an important thing you learned in your study preparation this week or while reading the assigned chapter.
3. Discuss your answers to questions 2-6.
4. What is a conviction?
5. How can you discern between a scriptural conviction and one derived only from background and prejudice?
6. How should we express our convictions? Should we attempt to change others to our way of thinking?
7. Talk about your answers to questions 7-9.
8. Discuss the memory verse and the special project.
9. Close in group prayer.

Suggested Scripture Memory: Acts 17:11

Special Project: Make a list of major areas in which you have developed convictions you feel are biblical. Make another list of areas in which you desire to develop more personal convictions. After you have done this, share your lists with a mature Christian you trust, and ask for comments and suggestions.

BIBLIOGRAPHY

———————⁓———————

Andrews, Kenneth R. "Ethics in Practice." *Harvard Business Review*. (September/October 1989): 99.

Chewning, Richard C., ed. *Principles and Business: The Foundations*. Colorado Springs: NavPress, 1989.

____. *Principles and Economics: The Foundations*. Colorado Springs: NavPress, 1989.

____. *Principles and Business: The Practice*. Colorado Springs: NavPress, 1990.

____. *Principles and Public Policy: The Practice*. Colorado Springs: NavPress, 1990.

Colson, Charles W. "Right or Wrong in Today's Society." Speech given at Harvard Business School, 4 April 1991. *Vital Speeches of the Day*. (1991): 556-562.

Freudberg, David. *The Corporate Conscience: Money, Power, and Responsible Business*. New York: AMACOM, A Division of the American Management Association, 1986.

Liebig, James E. *Business Ethics: Profiles in Civic Virtue*. Denver: Fulcrum, 1990.

Madsen, Peter, and Shafritz, Jay M., ed. *Essentials in Business Ethics: A Collection of Articles*. New York: Meridian (Penguin), 1990

MacArthur, John. *The Vanishing Conscience: Drawing the Line in a No Fault, Guilt Free World*. Dallas, Tex.: Word, 1994.

Nash, Laura. *Good Intentions Aside: A Manager's Guide to Resolving Ethical Problems*. Boston: Harvard Business School Press, 1990.

Tamasy, Robert J., ed. *The Complete Christian Businessman*. Brentwood, Tenn.: Wolgemuth & Hyatt, Publishers; CBMC, USA, 1991.

AUTHOR

Dr. Jerry White is the president and chief executive officer of The Navigators and is responsible for the worldwide operation of The Navigators. The Navigators have more than 3,550 staff ministering in ninety-five countries, working with college students, military personnel, business and professional people, and churches.

Dr. White was born in Iowa and raised in Spokane, Washington. He attended the University of Washington and received a B.S. in electrical engineering in 1959. In 1964 he received a Masters Degree in Astronautics from The Air Force Institute of Technology. He earned his Ph.D. in Astronautics from Purdue University in 1970.

Following his graduation from the University of Washington, Dr. White received a commission in the U.S. Air Force. During his thirteen years of active duty he served in many capacities, including an assignment as a mission controller at Cape Kennedy during the height of the American space program. He also was an associate professor of astronautics at the Air Force Academy in Colorado for six years and has coauthored a nationally recognized textbook on astrodynamics. Dr. White resigned from active service in 1973 but continues to serve as a major general in the Air Force Reserves.

Dr. White is a registered professional engineer, a member of the Tau Beta Pi Honorary Engineering Society, and an associate fellow of the American Institute of Aeronautics and Astronautics. In 1991 and from 1993 to 1995 he served as chairman of the Colorado Rhodes Scholarship Selection Committee.

Dr. White first came into contact with The Navigators as a student at the University of Washington. Throughout his military career he maintained close contact with The Navigators, beginning the organization's ministries at the Air Force Academy and Purdue University. He served in several leadership roles with The Navigators. He became president and general director in 1986.

In addition to his work with The Navigators, Dr. White is an avid handball player, a licensed commercial pilot, and an active member of his local church, having served on the church board. He and his wife, Mary, have four children (the eldest, Steve, died in 1990), nine grandchildren, and live in Colorado Springs, Colorado.

Dr. White has written several books, including *The Power of Commitment*, and *Friends and Friendship* (with Mary). Mary is the author of *Harsh Grief, Gentle Hope* (NavPress, 1995). The following titles are available through Singapore NavPress: *On the Job: Survival or Satisfaction?* and *Making the Grade*. Contact the Castle Bookstore, Glen Eyrie Conference Center, P.O. Box 6000, Colorado Springs, CO 80934.